Rig Your Dinghy Right

Rig Your Dinghy Right

John Hodgart and Mark Chisnell

International Marine
Camden, Maine

Published by International Marine,
an imprint of McGraw-Hill, Inc.

First published in Great Britain
by Waterline Books
an imprint of Airlife Publishing Ltd
10 9 8 7 6 5 4 3 2 1

ISBN 0-07-029123-3

Questions regarding the content of this book
should be addressed to:
International Marine
P.O. Box 220
Camden, ME 04843
Questions regarding the ordering of this book
should be addressed to:
TAB Books, A Division of McGraw-Hill, Inc.
Blue Ridge Summit, PA 17294
1-800-233-1128

Acknowledgements

The authors would like to thank Racing Sailboats Ltd., Paul Brotherton of Hyde Sails, Mark Rushall of Proctor Masts, Paul Young of Rondar Boats and all the other individuals who allowed their boats to be photographed. Not to mention everyone at Claydon Heeley International who put up with us taking over half their office!

Contents

Part Two

Introduction

This is a book about dinghy systems, the paraphernalia of pulleys, ropes, cleats, wire, shackles, screws, bolts and nuts that turn a dinghy from a wooden or composite plastic structure into a functioning sailing machine.

The book is divided into two halves. Part One consists of chapters 1 to 4, and here you will find advice on the general aspects of dinghy systems. How to fasten fittings in place, overall design considerations, how to use pulleys and levers to generate a specific mechanical advantage, and how to choose the right fittings for the job. In Part Two we move along to more specific systems, and this is the place to look if you are trying to improve a particular part of the boat's equipment.

What the book will not do is tell you why and when you should or should not be pulling any of your newly efficient control lines. There are plenty of good books on boat tuning for speed. But this one is about making your dinghy work - the first step to winning races. You cannot sail the boat fast if the basic tuning controls do not work efficiently.

Hopefully it will be useful to a variety of people, from those who have spent an entire year pulling on the vang with virtually no effect on the leech profile, through to the owner/builder of a fourth International 14 who has still not found a mainsheet system he is happy with. If you have a boat that does not quite work the way you want it to, then this is the book for you. And for those considering fitting out a boat from the bare or part-fitted hull - you should be able to find everything here to help. From decisions such as how you are going to hold up and control the mast, through to ensuring enough purchase in control lines and keeping fittings screwed on and water-tight.

We wish you many happy and productive hours of boat bimbling.

MC and JH

Part One

Chapter 1

Fastenings

All systems and components of a racing dinghy are attached to the hull. This chapter aims to cover some of the multitude of different methods of achieving this. It will also give some guidance on the actual positioning and alignment of fittings in relation to each other to ensure they have least chance of pulling off and can work to their best efficiency.

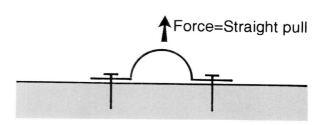

1.1: Straight pull on a fitting is in the direction of the fastenings.

General Principles

When choosing methods of fastening components to the hull there are several considerations. The role of the component is important, for example the shroud anchorage on any dinghy is one of the most highly loaded fittings and if this pulls out or fails the mast will almost certainly go overboard - it's difficult to finish a race with no rig! Conversely if the final lead block on the jib cunningham control pulls out you may lose a few boat lengths, but it is not going to be catastrophic unless it is holding you on-board at the time.

In an ideal world nothing would pull off, but to optimise weight distribution, position and looks sometimes you have to compromise. So when fastening equipment to the hull the considerations must be:
1. Keep the rig in the boat.
2. Keep the crew on board.
3. Maintain full adjustment.

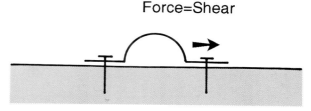

1.2: Shear force is at right angles to the fastenings.

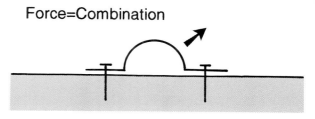

1.3: Combination force is where the applied load has both a straight and shear component.

Forces

The direction of force on a fitting relative to the fixing surface is an important consideration and there are three different types, straight pull, shear and combination (see Illustrations 1.1, 1.2 and 1.3).

The magnitude of the force and whether the fitting will be subjected to shock loading must also be considered. For example the shock loading on the mainsheet strops whilst gybing in 20 knots of wind is much larger than the static forces generated whilst sailing to windward in the same breeze. A further consideration,

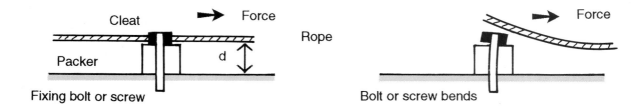

1.4: *This shows how the shear force on the cleat is magnified by the packing, with the consequence that the bolts have bent and released the sheet. The actual force on the bolts/screws is multiplied by the distance 'd'. The bigger 'd' is (ie. the higher the cleat) the more the force on the fasteners and the more chance the cleat will tilt and release the rope.*

especially in the case of cleats, is the lever effect of the force on the fitting. For example, cam cleats are often mounted on high packing wedges to enable the cleat to be used more easily. The effect of this is illustrated in 1.4, where the lever effect from the force has released the cleat. The fixing bolts or screws bend under the magnified load and cause the cleat to misalign and release the rope.

Materials

Always use stainless steel screws, bolts and nuts as they are stronger and will resist the dreaded corrosion of the marine environment. If you need to check, stainless is not magnetic. There are two common grades of stainless material available, 304 for above the waterline and 316 for below. Type 316 is better as it has higher anti-corrosive properties, but it costs more. Type 304 is generally acceptable for use anywhere on a racing dinghy, as these boats are rarely kept permanently afloat and they are always hosed or washed down after use - are they not? Type 304 may rust slightly on the surface causing slight discolouration but this can easily be removed and does not weaken the fastening.

Aluminium alloy is also used extensively in racing dinghies on masts, booms, poles, rudder stocks, tillers, centreboards, brackets etc. Although most of it is anodised, when it is in direct contact with stainless steel an electrolytic reaction is set up in the presence of water and this causes accelerated corrosion mainly to the aluminium. This tends to result in the enlargement of fastener holes which cause the fitting to fall off. In order to minimise this effect the two materials must be insulated from each other.

The best material for this is zinc chromate paste, a yellow substance used by most quality mast manufacturers. This must be smeared onto the surface of stainless fittings, and screws and bolts must be dipped in the paste before fastening to aluminium. Zinc chromate is available from well stocked chandlers but if it is unavailable most types of sealant will do the job reasonably satisfactorily.

With carbon fibre composites being used in ever more applications it is important to note that carbon has a very corrosive reaction when in contact with any metal in the presence of water. As a consequence it is essential to try to insulate the two materials when dealing with carbon and metal.

Types of Fastening

Most fittings are held to the hull using one of the following methods; screws, bolts, rivets or glue. The method employed depends on several factors; into/onto what material, location, magnitude and direction of load.

Screws

Screws fall into two categories, wood screws and self tappers. These can then have two different shapes of head; pan head or countersunk and two different types of drive, slotted or cross-head. These are all shown in

1.5: Types of screw, top left is a wood screw with a countersunk head, then a self tapper with a pan head and self tapper with a countersunk head. Below is a cross, or Phillip's, head on the left and a slot head on the right.

1.6: A self tapper screwing a fitting into the thin wall of an aluminium tube - we can see how important it is that the thread goes all the way to the top of the screw.

illustration 1.5. Self tappers are usually the most useful as they have the widest number of applications. Because the thread goes all the way to the head they can be used when screwing fittings into thin materials (Illustration 1.6). The choice of pan head or countersunk is usually dictated by the fitting and whether a flush mounting, for example on keel bands, is required. Slotted screws are the most common but the use of cross-heads is becoming more

widespread as they are much easier to use with power screwdrivers (there is less chance of the screwdriver bit slipping off the screw head).

When using self tapping screws it is important to drill pilot holes of the right size and this obviously depends on the size of screw and the material being self-tapped into. If the hole is too small the material, especially wood, may split as the screw is forced in or you may shear off the screw head if the screw locks up (this is more likely to happen in aluminium). If the pilot hole is too big the screw will not bite properly and the thread you have made will strip too easily. As usual a compromise must be reached. The table shown in illustration 1.7 will give some guidance to pilot holes but it is always advisable to try a few test holes in some scrap material first. Ideally you want to drill the minimum size hole so the screw has maximum grip.

Pilot Hole Size

Screw Size	Soft Wood		Hard Wood/Alloy	
	Imperial	Metric	Imperial	Metric
4	5/64"	2.0mm	7/64"	2.5mm
6	7/64"	2.5mm	1/8"	3.0mm
8	1/8"	3.0mm	9/64"	3.5mm
10	9/64"	3.5mm	5/32"	4.0mm
12	5/32"	4.0mm	11/64"	4.5mm

1.7: Table of drill sizes for self tapping screws.

If a screw is proving difficult to tap into a material, rather than just drill a bigger hole you can try using a lubricant on the screw. Smear a little grease on the start of the thread or scrape the thread on a bar of soap. If you are using a sealant, that will often lubricate the screw. It is easier to shear the heads off smaller screws (sizes 4, 6 and 8) so try to take more care when using these. Also be careful not to overtighten screws as this may strip the thread. If you do strip the thread, usually the only solution is to move up a screw size, although sometimes you can fill the hole with epoxy and start again (time consuming, as you have to wait for the epoxy to set hard).

If you shear the head off a screw it is best to remove the remaining part of the screw by taking off the fitting you were attaching. You can then grip the protruding part of the screw with a pair of vise grips to remove it. Always use as long a screw as possible to get maximum grip. If you are self tapping into pads attached to the hull and you do not want to pierce the outside skin with your pilot hole, mark the depth on the drill bit with a piece of adhesive tape and then drill in to your mark (Illustration 1.8).

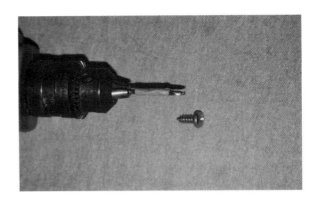

1.8: With any fitting attached from the inside of the hull outer skin it is important not to pierce the hull when drilling the pilot hole for the screw. You can mark the drill bit with tape to ensure that you only drill as far as the screw needs to go in - you should have already checked that the screw is not too long.

Self Tapping Into Wood

Drill a pilot hole appropriate to the hardness and depth of the wood and use a sealant. But try not to use silicone based sealants on wood because if you want to repaint or revarnish the boat small traces of silicone can be left even after a good rubbing down. These will cause 'fish eye' blemishes in the paint or varnish finish.

Self Tapping into Solid Glassfibre

The size of the pilot hole is critical if you do not want to crack the surrounding gel coat. It is best to drill a test hole in a scrap piece of laminate or if this is impractical drill your pilot hole slightly oversize through the gelcoat layer (Illustration 1.9).

Pilot hole oversize through gel coat

Gel coat

Glass fibre

1.9: An oversize pilot hole through the gel coat layer will ensure that you do not crack it when screwing the fitting on.

Self Tapping into Foam Sandwich

Many modern dinghies are constructed using composites where there is a glass/foam/glass sandwich laminate (Illustration 1.10). This forms strong, light and stiff panels but is difficult to attach fittings to as the foam is usually of a low density and will not provide any grip for the screw. The best approach here is to replace the foam locally with wood or an epoxy/filler mix. Then you can self tap into the more solid laminate, or you can bolt through without fear of crushing the foam core and distorting the glass surfaces. To replace the foam with wood the top glass laminate and the foam core beneath it must be removed. A wooden core plug must

Glass

Foam

Glass

1.10: Glassfibre sandwich using a foam middle layer.

now be shaped to the same size and thickness as the original foam piece. This wood plug must now be glued in position and the top glass laminate replaced and finished to match the

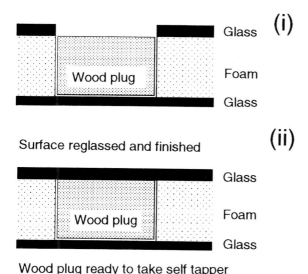

(i) Glass / Foam / Glass

Surface reglassed and finished

(ii) Glass / Foam / Glass

Wood plug ready to take self tapper

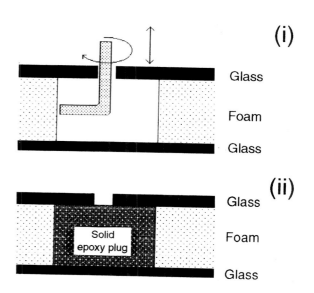

(i) Glass / Foam / Glass

(ii) Glass / Foam / Glass

1.11: To provide a solid backing to attach fittings to, a wooden plug can be used to replace the foam locally.

existing surface (illustration 1.11).

This is a time consuming method and it is often difficult to match the original surface (especially if it is a gel coat). But it is secure and a good method of reinforcing a foam/glass laminate to take high loads. Of course if you can get to the inside surface, which is not normally seen, then the job is much easier as the final finish on the inside of the wooden block is not of any great concern.

An alternative to using a wood plug is to use an epoxy/filler mix. The method here is to drill a hole through the top glass layer into the foam, being careful not to drill into the second glass layer. Then insert a bent nail or similar through your top hole and twist using a very slow speed drill. This will crush and clear a hollow disc in the foam between the two layers of glass. When this is cleared prepare a liquid mixture of epoxy and filler and inject this into the top hole, using a syringe, until you fill the void. Let the epoxy go off and you now have a solid disc of epoxy into which you can self tap (Illustration 1.12).

1.12: An alternative to using the wooden block is to clear the foam with a bent nail on a slow speed drill, then syringe an epoxy/filler mixture into the cavity.

Self Tapping into Alloy

You should again test to ensure that you have the correct size pilot hole. Always lubricate and always use an insulating sealant like zinc chromate.

Bolts and Nuts

Bolts are probably one of the safest and most reliable methods of attachment. Bolts and machined screws come with the same variety of heads as screws, plus the additional hexagonal head for use with a spanner, or wrench.

Always try to use nylocks or locknuts on bolts as this minimizes the risk of the nut loosening or pulling off. This is especially important on boats that are regularly trailed, as the vibration caused by trailering often loosens ordinary nuts. If neither are obtainable, then use one of the 'Loctite' type glues that are available. Try not to use epoxy as this often leads to problems when trying to remove nuts to replace worn or damaged fittings.

The diameter of the bolt or machined screw is

usually dictated by the fitting being used. If in doubt most fittings can be drilled out to size - within reason. A common problem exists between European manufactured fittings, usually suitable for M5 (5mm) diameter bolts, and US manufactured fittings designed to suit 3/16" diameter bolts. The 3/16" holes are not quite big enough for M5 bolts so here the solution is to run a 5mm drill through the existing holes. But remember that stainless steel is a very hard material so when drilling it use sharp drills and a light lubricating oil such as WD40.

When using bolts the security of the fitting is dependant on the panel stiffness of the hull material so it is often wise to use backing plates, pads or large penny washers to spread the load when bolting into thin plywood or fibreglass. Also ensure you can reach the nut side of the bolt before you drill your holes. Usually if you are bolting through a bulkhead or into a buoyancy tank there is limited access to the other side of the bolt and this may limit where you can position certain fittings.

When you have difficulty with access to the other side of a fitting, to hold or locate the nut you can use the 'stick and sight method'. You use the correct size ring spanner for the nut and tape the other side of the ring to hold the nut in position (Illustration 1.13). Then tape the spanner to a piece of wood or batten so that you can now reach further than the length of your arm. Get someone to sight through the hole you have already drilled for the fitting and they can tell you when you have the nut in the correct position - don't move! Carefully screw the bolt into the nut to get it started. Now take away the spanner and stick and remove the tape. It can then be used as an extended spanner to tighten the bolt up on the fitting.

Bolts are often too long and ideally the excess should be cut off after they have been attached, but this is sometimes impossible. If you have to cut down a bolt before it is used, first run a nut onto it, clamp the excess end in a vice and hacksaw it off to the correct length. Then clean up the cut end with a file and run the nut back off the bolt to realign any bent or damaged threads. Some boat builders use captive nuts, usually glassed or glued into place

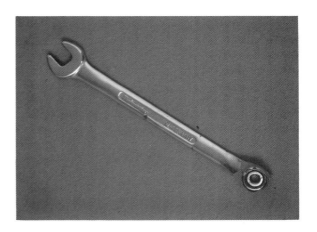

1.13: The 'stick and sight' method, using a nut taped into place in a spanner (wrench), useful where access is difficult or out of reach.

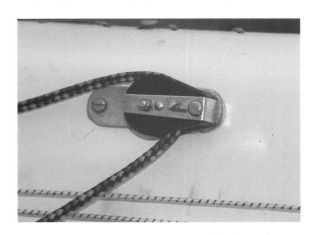

1.14: A new cheek block attached where the holes did not match those of the original fitting. The new block has been attached to an aluminium plate which has holes drilled to match the originals. Note the middle fixing is a nut on the bolt fastened from underneath.

prior to bonding the deck moulding to the hull moulding. This is fine until you want to replace it with another fitting with different hole spacings. One way round this is to make up a mounting plate for your fitting which makes use of the captive bolts, as in illustration 1.14. Here a cheek block is to be mounted and the hole spacings do not match. The solution is to pre-drill the plate (6mm alloy) to match the captive bolts then use one of these holes as a common

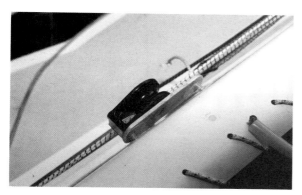

1.15: *The same fitting as in 1.14, you can see the countersunk bolt going through from the underside.*

fixing hole and drill the other hole common to the fitting through the thin plate and attach by using a countersunk bolt fixed from the underside (Illustration 1.15).

Rivets

Most rivets used on sailing dinghies are pop rivets. The rivet is put in a blind hole and the mandrel is withdrawn causing the blind part of the rivet to expand until it is flush with the fixing surface. At this point the mandrel head shears off (with a pop!) leaving the long mandrel in the rivet gun and the rounded head in the rivet (Illustration 1.16).

Pop rivets are usually aluminium or monel (there are some stainless steel ones but these are difficult to 'pull' because the stainless is so hard). In most cases it is best to use monel rivets as these are stronger. Always knock out the mandrel heads from the rivets as these are usually steel and will corrode in a marine environment. The head can be knocked out by inserting a thin punch, or the old mandrel, through the rivet.

The most common use for rivets is to attach fittings to masts or thin walled alloy tubes but they can also be used on thin fibreglass panels. When using on thin fibreglass, for example when fixing hatch covers, try to use aluminium rivets as these require less force to pop, and so will not crush the fibreglass.

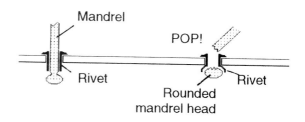

Before pulling   After pulling

1.16: *The pop rivet, showing how the rounded mandrel head pulls the rivet out to form the fastening.*

a

b

c

1.17: *Sometimes the rivet cannot be pushed in flush because of the shape of the fitting (a). The solution to this is to use a tube to extend the rivet gun head (b) and (c), but this will only work up to a point as eventually the mandrel slips out from the jaws of the rivet gun.*

When using rivets drill the appropriate diameter hole to match the rivet and ensure the fitting is held flush with its fixing surface prior to pulling the rivet. Check the clearance of the pop rivet gun-head as you may find that you cannot push the rivet in flush as the head of the gun is dislodged by the fitting (Illustration 1.17). This can sometimes be overcome by using a small piece of tubing or washers.

Glue and Glass

Modern glues and epoxies are highly effective and this may be an appropriate method of fixing, especially in the case of slot gaskets or keelbands. Sometimes to enable a fitting to be sited in the best place you may have to glue on a pad of wood, then attach the fitting to that. An even stronger method of fitting pads to a surface is to glue on the wood then glass it in place (Illustration 1.18). This method relies on using the glued area to spread the load over a large surface so the area of the pad in contact with the surface must be appropriate to the load on the fittings. For example you must use an area of approximately 100mm x 100mm to attach toe strap anchor points to.

Most glue or epoxy manufacturers have good, clear instructions for the use of their products and these must be followed carefully to ensure you get the strongest possible bond. In general both surfaces must be dry, usually lightly abraded, and free from any grease or paint. Also, especially with epoxies there is often a minimum temperature at which they will cure. Care must be taken to mix the correct quantities with two-part substances.

Knot and Hole

Finally a simple method of attachment which can be forgotten when faced with the blinding array of eyes, loops, plates, etc. Drill a hole through the fixing surface and thread a piece of rope or string through it and tie a stopper knot (Illustration 1.19)

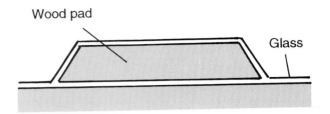

1.18: A wooden pad glued and glassed in place.

1.19: The simplest form of fastening, a knot and a hole!

Chapter 2

Designing the Systems

There are three areas for consideration when designing the control systems for a dinghy (and a lot of other things to take into account, but we will come on to that shortly). Initially you need to decide what type of rig you are going to have, and with what devices you are going to control the rake and bend of the mast. Having got that sorted you need to decide on the sail control systems; some things are obvious, you certainly need a mainsheet, but what type? Do you need a spinnaker chute? Or a fly-away pole? These things must be decided at the outset and at least an overall list, if not a sketch of the design of the boat's systems established. This gives you the best chance of not finding, for instance, that your fly-away pole system will not work because you have put the mast strut in the way.

Type of Rig and Control Systems

The biggest decision here would be the type of rig, but it almost certainly will not be your decision to make, since the class rules will determine it for you. There are two commonly used types of dinghy rig, the Una rig; such as the Finn or the Laser, and the sloop rig; as on the Fireball, 470, 505 or Mirror. Most mainsails will be bermudan rigged rather than gaff rigged. Although gaff rigs can be seen on some spectacularly popular boats, such as the Sunfish and the Mirror, its use is part of the class rules. Apart from hoisting the mainsail on a gaff, there is little difference in the considerations when designing the boat's systems. The biggest difference is on the sloop rig, you have spreaders with a bermudan main, but not usually with a gaff, so mast bend in the upper third will only be controlled by the gaff itself. Which is why Mirror sailors spend hours planing down gaffs to match mainsail luff curve.

Una Rig

Let us assume first that you are using a una rig without standing rigging, in which case there are two ways of stepping the mast. The first, which is most commonly seen on the Laser dinghy, is a fixed tube into which the mast slots (Illustration 2.1). This is about the simplest way possible to rig a boat. There is no standing rigging and no mast bend control. Your only further considerations are the mainsail controls of sheet, halyard, cunningham, outhaul and vang.

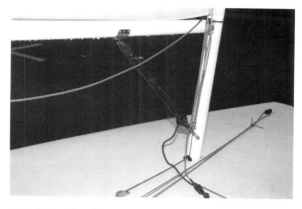

2.1: *The simplest way to step a una rig, slot the mast into a tube in the deck.*

The second, and more sophisticated way of doing it, is to step the mast on the hog and then fix it some distance above, usually at deck level. This is the system that you see in the Finn, Optimist and Europe dinghies (Illustration 2.2). It allows you to control the mast rake, and hence the available power from the sail, by moving either the heel of the mast, or the fixed point above it. If it is possible to do either then the simplest solution is to adjust the mast foot along a rack arrangement. The disadvantage to this is that it is difficult to alter it while you are racing. It would be possible to design a system that could move the mast foot whilst the rig is under load, but rake adjustment on the water is

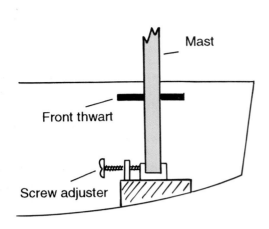

2.2: *The mast stepping system on the Optimist, which allows you to change the rake and bend by moving the mast foot in comparison to the fixed point higher up. The same basic principle is applied by the Finn and the Europe.*

best provided by controlling the mast at deck level.

Una rigs with standing rigging, have similar problems to sloop rigs with standing rigging, which we will consider next.

Sloop Rig

The sloop rig can be divided into two basic types, the deck-stepped mast (Illustration 2.3) and the hog-stepped version (Illustration 2.4). Much of the mechanics of the two types is the same. They are both held up with two shrouds and a forestay or jib wire. Anything else, spreaders, lowers, diamonds and struts, to name but some of the possibilities, are more about controlling the mast rake and bend than actually holding it up. The differences are marginal, firstly, you have less mast in the boat, so the all-up weight is lower. Less obviously, when the rake is changed on a deck-stepped mast, the pivot point (the heel) should be at the same vertical height as the base point of the shrouds, which helps to maintain the geometry of the spreaders. If you adjust the rake on a deck-stepped mast you have to re-adjust the spreaders much less to maintain the same deflection and hence mast bend. This

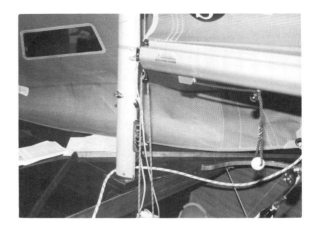

2.3: *The deck-stepped sloop rig, seen on an Enterprise.*

2.4: *The hog-stepped sloop rig, seen on a 470.*

difference makes an important aspect of boat tuning much simpler. With the variables of rake and spreader position no longer interacting, mast bend can be altered independently of rake, and vice versa, with just one adjustment. Finally, and of rather more obvious practical concern, if you break the jib halyard you will not break a deck-stepped mast.

Despite these differences the controls required for each rig are the same. In an ideal world you should at least design your dinghy's systems so that you have some means of adjusting the mast foot position, the mast bend at the goose neck or deck level, the mast rake, the tension applied to the forestay or jib halyard, and the spreader angle. On top of this you then decide if you need a second set of spreaders, jumpers or diamonds. But what emphasis you put on all this equipment depends on what sort of rig you are trying to develop.

You need an overall concept of what rig type it is you want, and this can most easily come through discussion with your sailmaker. If the class is well-established and you are buying the latest sails from a popular loft then they should be able to tell you what kind of mast rake and bend control you need. In the absence of such advice you have two choices of rig, bent and straight. The bent rig relies on the mast bending to depower, the straight rig does it by raking back (often the fastest rigs, as in the 470, use a combination of both). For the first you will need more efficient control of the mast bend, through a strut perhaps, than you will of the shroud position and hence rake. The opposite applies for the straight rig. When it comes to making a choice between the two, in general the bent rig is a more automatic rig. The mast will bend and alter the set-up to comply with changing conditions on its own. In contrast the straight rig requires adjustment to match the rake to changing conditions of wind strength and waves.

Sail Controls

So much for mast bend and rake, what about the power unit of the boat, what devices are you going to use to trim the sails? The foresail, be it jib or genoa, is relatively straightforward. You will certainly need to adjust the sheet lead position, do you want to move it both fore and aft as well as athwartships? You will also need to consider where the control lines for the adjustment lead. For a two sail boat barber haulers are also a consideration, because without a spinnaker the jib has a much increased importance downwind. For some classes a self-tacking facility or a furler may be an option. The final tweak is usually a jib cunningham.

The mainsail gives much more scope for the imagination. There are nearly as many mainsheet systems as there are classes; from the straight-forward aft or centre mainsheets, through various hoops and struts. Which you choose will have an impact both on the way you sail the boat and the rest of the systems that you require. If you use a traveller you will not need such an effective vang for instance. For each of the vang, cunningham and the outhaul, you need to decide both on the amount of purchase, where the purchase will run and where the control line leads.

Finally there is the spinnaker. If it is symmetric then you need to decide on whether it is going to have some kind of fly-away or twin pole system, or the detachable sort that goes in the bottom of the boat. Again this may well be controlled by the class rules, the 470 insists on a completely detachable pole for instance. The sheet system, and particularly the inclusion of twinning lines needs thought, as does where you are going to retrieve it to, a bag or a chute. The halyard is the final piece of equipment, be it a 1:2 purchase, pump action or straight pull with a take up. Much the same goes for an asymmetric, if anything, because of the increased size of the sail, the systems will need to be even more efficient.

Further Considerations

As we have already mentioned, you are unlikely to be making the decisions on the type of rig and control systems, as discussed above, in a completely free environment. There will be constraints, the biggest of which is probably going to be the class rules of the dinghy in question.

Class Rules

Be it a strict one-design or a restricted rule development class, there will almost certainly be some constraints on how you rig your dinghy imposed by the class association. For something like the Laser, you have virtually no choice in how the boat is fitted out. At the other extreme, the International 14 allows you control right down to the main/foresail area ratios. But whatever class of boat it is you would be foolish to do any work on it without having spent some time studying the latest class rules.

Budget

The budget is a big factor for most of us, and it should be taken into account from the top down. Decide where you need the most efficient systems and spend the money there first. You may decide you prefer a simple centre mainsheet system with a couple of fixed bridles. In which case as soon as the wind gets up you will be dependent on a strong vang to keep the leech tension. Spending some of the money saved, by not getting a traveller, on an efficient ball-bearing vang system would be good budgeting. Whereas if you have gone for the full-length, ball-bearing traveller, a cheaper lever vang may well be appropriate.

Always buy the more expensive ball bearing blocks and cleats for the high load areas where you can. For instance you will probably get away with a plastic cam cleat on the jib cunningham, but the same fitting for the vang tail is a false economy - it will not last two minutes.

The Crew

The people that will sail the boat with you are a big consideration. Their physical size, strength and sailing ability all play a part in the type of systems that you need. If you are going to pick up forward hands out of the dinghy park for most of the season it is as well to lead back the sail controls to the helm. Keep the front end as simple as possible for the novices. But if you are about to do your first year in International 14's with an experienced crew who also happens to be your sailmaker, then you might as well lead it all to him at the front end so he can get on with the sail trim while you concentrate on steering the boat - and keeping it upright. Similarly whether to put ratchets on the jib and spinnaker sheets will depend on how strong the crew is. And whether to go for the extra weight and complexity of a twin or fly-away spinnaker pole will depend on their dexterity through the hoists, gybes and drops.

Reliability

You do not win races sitting on the beach fixing your boat. The system should always be up to the job that you are asking it to do. This means careful attention to aspects that we discuss in more detail elsewhere, the strength and type of fitting, and the way it is fastened to the boat. It also means maintenance, you should never go into any event without thoroughly checking the boat if you want to win. See if anything is coming loose, that blocks still spin and cleats still jam.

Simple Works

The KIS principle is as valuable in yacht racing as anywhere else. *Keep It Simple*. Adding blocks, cleats and rope adds weight, cost and risk of failure. The more you have on your boat the more there is to break (Illustration 2.5). David Barnes won three 470 World Championships with a boat that was so simple it would have looked basic at a sailing school. But it all worked, and it suited his style.

Other People's Ideas

We have yet to see a dinghy control system that was patented or copyrighted. The most prolific source of good ideas for your boat, apart from this book, are other people's boats. And not just in your own fleet either. What is now the almost standard mainsheet system in the British Lark fleet was borrowed from a 470, and arrived there modified from the Fireballs, who pinched it from the Laser and so it goes on....

2.5: *The more equipment there is, the more there is to break.*

Planning and Mock-Ups

Before you go on to choose specific fittings you must plan each system carefully so it can be accommodated in your boat and will not foul anything else. If you mock-up all the new systems by marking fitting positions on pieces of masking tape this may prevent you having to make embarrassing attempts at gelcoat repairs!

Within each system, no matter whether it is the rig tension control or a simple led-aft mainsail cunningham, the efficiency of the whole depends on all the component blocks and parts being able to align with each other. There is no point in buying expensive ball bearing blocks if you attach them so that they do not articulate in the right direction and the rope drags on the cheeks instead of running around the sheave. When fixing blocks in position have a short piece of shock cord or line to mock-up the direction the rope will go through. Then drill and attach just one fixing point on the deck loop or fitting so that it can be swivelled to locate where to drill the other fixing hole. Have a look at how the deck loops are angled in illustration 2.6.

Make sure you have enough room for each of your systems. There are usually many control lines running aft from the base of the mast in particular. It takes careful planning to ensure everything can be led back at the correct angle in this area (Illustration 2.7).

2.6: *You should attach blocks so that there is a clean lead of the rope into and away from the turn. These are particularly neat since the line of the block almost bisects the angle the rope turns through.*

2.7: *The foot of the mast is invariably the most complex area of the boat, as a consequence it also needs the greatest amount of planning.*

Time

Try to make sure you have enough time. As a rule of thumb, most 'ten minute jobs' take about two hours, and the average 'couple of hours work' takes all day!

Hopefully this chapter has indicated the lines you should be thinking along, and the questions you should be asking before considering any changes to your dinghy systems. The rest of the book should answer those questions.

Chapter 3

Some Mechanical Principles

Almost all the systems on your dinghy use some kind of mechanical advantage to reduce the loads to a manageable level. It would not be possible, for instance, for you to pull the boom down with a directly attached piece of rope. Instead you use a mechanical system, such as a pulley or a lever, to reduce the load to a level where you can pull it comfortably. But nothing in life, and certainly not in physics, is for free, and by the same proportion that you lower the load, you increase the distance that you must pull it. This keeps the amount of work done constant, and nature happy by complying with the Law of Conservation of Energy.

The lever is the simplest mechanical system that allows you to alter a load to a manageable form. We need to know a little about the moment of a force about a point to understand how a lever works. A moment being the ability of a force to produce rotation, and not surprisingly it is the product of the force and its distance from the point of rotation. Illustration 3.1 shows a simple lever in action. This is actually the fundamental principle by which both levers and pulleys work, as we shall see shortly. The ratio of the load to the effort, which here is L/E, is known as the mechanical advantage. In the real world where friction exists, it will always be slightly less than in our ideal example.

Mechanical Advantage = $\dfrac{\text{Load}}{\text{Effort}}$

We can also see the justification for our earlier comments about nothing being for free. Although the load is moved with less effort, it has to travel further by an amount called the transmission factor or velocity ratio:

Transmission Factor = $\dfrac{\text{Distance moved against load}}{\text{Distance moved by effort}}$

Which in illustration 3.1 we can show by trigonometry to be b/a. In fact if we ignore friction it is always the inverse of the mechanical advantage. Which is why many people (including the rest of this book) talk about the mechanical advantage when they mean the inverse of the transmission factor - the two are reversible in frictionless worlds. But despite the best efforts of modern equipment manufacturers we have not quite reached this state of affairs yet. In the meantime the relationship of the mechanical advantage to the transmission factor is an indication of the efficiency of the system, 100% efficiency would mean that:

Mechanical Advantage = 1/Transmission Factor.

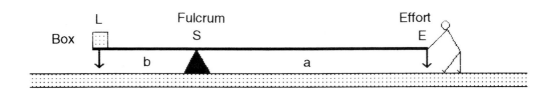

3.1: *The mechanics of a simple lever. The applied effort to lift the box is acting clockwise, whilst the box with the assistance of gravity wants to go anti-clockwise. The two moments are balanced and so (assuming the frictionless world all-to-familiar to physics students): E x a = L x b*
From the diagram and the equation we can see that a large load can be lifted with a smaller effort provided that 'a' is a bigger distance than 'b'.

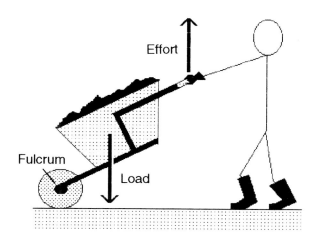

3.2: The second type of lever which has the load between the pivot point, or fulcrum, and the effort. As compared to 3.1 where the fulcrum is between the load and the effort.

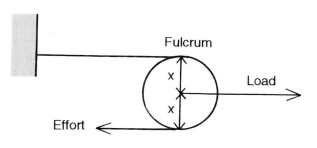

3.3: This shows how the pulley works on the same principle as the lever in illustration 3.2. The load splits the distance between the effort and the fulcrum in half so the transmission ratio is 1:2, and therefore the mechanical advantage is 2:1.

Using simple fairleads rather than ball bearing blocks could easily reduce a system with 1:4 transmission factor to a 2:1 mechanical advantage. For purchase systems the point is to keep them as friction free as possible.

There are two kinds of levers that interest us here, those like the one in illustration 3.1 with the pivot point, or fulcrum, between the load and the effort, and those as in illustration 3.2 where the load is between the fulcrum and the effort. Now we can see from illustration 3.3 why the pulley is another version of the lever - the second type, with the load between the fulcrum and the effort. Because the load splits the distance between the effort and the fulcrum in half, the transmission ratio is 1:2, and so the mechanical advantage of a single frictionless pulley is always 2:1 - a useful number to remember when we come to calculate these things later.

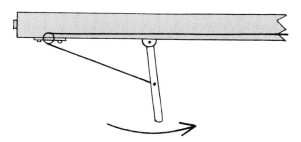

3.4: A lever used to tighten the outhaul, this is about the simplest application you will see of a lever.

Levers

So much for the physical principles, how does all this work in the real world of the dinghy? There are two common ways in which levers are used. The first applies the force directly by hand, as in illustration 3.4. It only has the two positions, on or off, and locks into place in the on position. One use for this type of lever is the outhaul. A little more sophisticated is the Highfield lever (Illustration 3.5) which is adjustable to the extent that the fulcrum can be moved further from the load. The disadvantage is that you have to ease it completely, by letting it off, to use this adjustment. Shroud levers also use direct force (Illustration 3.6), combined with a rack and clevis pin arrangement to provide adjustability. None of these levers provide much more than a 4:1 mechanical advantage, and in

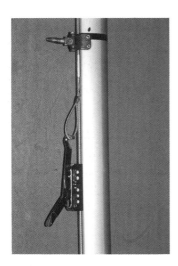

3.5: *The Highfield lever, a more sophisticated version of 3.4, which allows you to move the fulcrum point towards and away from the load. Moving it does give you some adjustment, but you have to completely release the load to use this facility.*

the case of a high load, like a shroud, this is hardly enough to provide easy adjustment. Most people have seen the dinghy park trick - you ask someone to let off the shroud levers and they barely escape with their fingers. Which is why it has become popular to combine the lever with a rope and pulley system - the second way in which they are used. This has the added advantage that the adjustment can be made from a distance, via the rope of the block and tackle. But before we embark on an explanation of these, we should first look at the pulley systems themselves.

Pulleys

There are also two ways of arranging pulleys and ropes to gain a mechanical advantage. The first is the block and tackle or multi-block system, where a single line runs back and forth between two sets of pulleys (Illustration 3.7). As we can see each pulley used increases the transmission factor by 1. The disadvantage is that you need a lot of blocks for any amount of purchase. The advantage of the system is that the set of pulleys only moves the same

a

b

3.6: *This type of shroud lever also provides a simple form of direct adjustment through the rack and pins. In (a) the lever is off, and in (b) the lever is on.*

distance as the load. You pull a lot more line out of the end of it, but the movement of the blocks is limited to that of the load. This makes it useful on jobs where a long travel is required.

A variation on this theme is the muscle box, which is a multi-block system housed in a case (Illustration 3.8). Their popularity is fading, due in part to the limits on travel imposed by the case, but also because the case provides additional friction. The same purchase can be

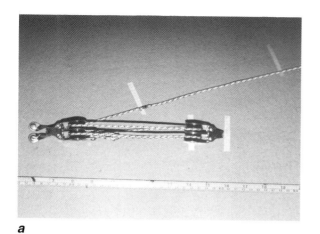
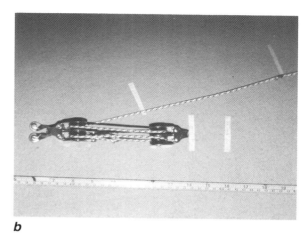

a **b**

3.7: *A 4:1 multi-block system. We can see how the pulleys travel as far as the load, which makes it useful where the available 'throw' or travel of the pulleys is limited. But it is expensive in terms of the number of blocks for a given mechanical advantage. The mark on the rope shows how four times as much rope is pulled out of the system as the load moves from (a) to (b).*

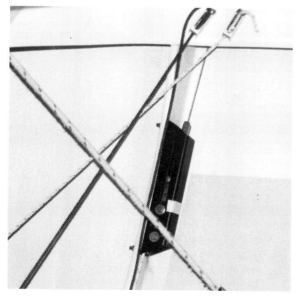

3.8: *Another version of the multi-block system, the muscle box. This is exactly the same inside as the system shown in 3.7. The number of pulleys will determine the mechanical advantage the box as a whole provides. The advantages are that it is neat, simple and easy to fit. The downside is that the case provides additional friction and therefore less efficiency, and the throw is limited to the length of the box.*

more efficiently achieved with a free-running system like that in illustration 3.7 - and only the length of the line limits the travel.

The second technique is the cascade system, which connects separate 2:1 rope and pulley sets (illustration 3.9). Each time you add another line and pulley you double the purchase. The cascade system gives you a lot more purchase for a lot less pulleys. Because there are fewer pulleys there will also be less friction and so the mechanical advantage will be higher for the same transmission factor. Its disadvantage is the movement of the blocks. The final block before the line emerges into the cleat will need to move half as far as the transmission factor for the whole system. So if it is a 1:16 transmission factor, for the load to move one inch the final block will need to move eight inches. You need a lot more space for travel than for the equivalent purchase on a multi-block system.

Fortunately the pros and cons of the two types of system dovetail, and if you cannot get what you want using just one system, you can usually combine cascades with multi-blocks to get just the right specification of travel and purchase. An example of this is seen in illustration 3.10 where a cascade is added to a multi-block. We have included some reference examples of multi-block and cascade purchase systems in illustration 3.11.

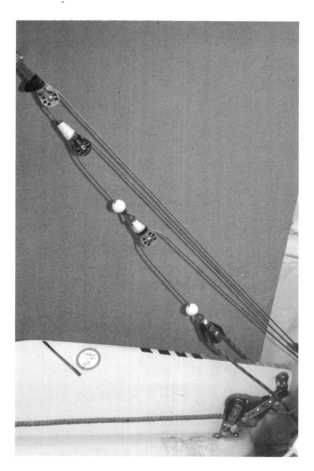

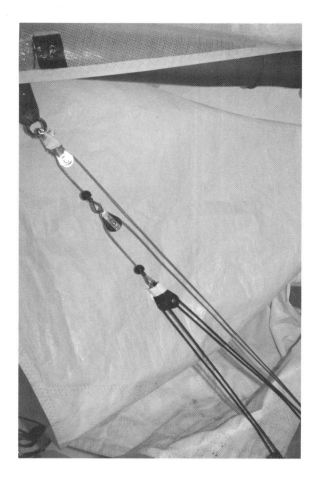

3.9: *A cascade system applied to a 470 kicker. Each successive 2:1 is fixed to the same base point, just out of the picture to the bottom right. The other end of the wire is then attached to a pulley which forms part of the next 2:1 purchase. Each successive 2:1 purchase added, doubles the total purchase of the system. Note the use of stopper bobbles which prevent the wire eye splice from being damaged when the system is let off.*

3.10: *This vang uses a cascade system initially, but because the amount of purchase required means that the blocks will bottom out before the necessary travel is achieved on the boom, it finishes with a multi-block system. This provides more purchase with less travel. Using the two types in a combination like this will usually achieve the required amount of travel and purchase.*

Pulleys and Levers

We can now return to the combination systems we mentioned earlier, that of pulleys and levers. In the same way that we used cascades and multi-blocks above, we can combine a lever with a block and tackle to meet the requirements of the job, as we can see in illustration 3.12.

A more specialised use can be seen in illustration 3.13, showing the lever used to chock a 470 mast at deck level. The class rules do not allow action at a distance, this combination of a lever acting directly on the mast at about 2:1 pulled with a 4:1 purchase provides, at 8:1, about the maximum mechanical advantage possible within the class rules. It is just enough to allow the ram to be pulled on upwind with the mainsheet and vang loads still acting in the opposite direction.

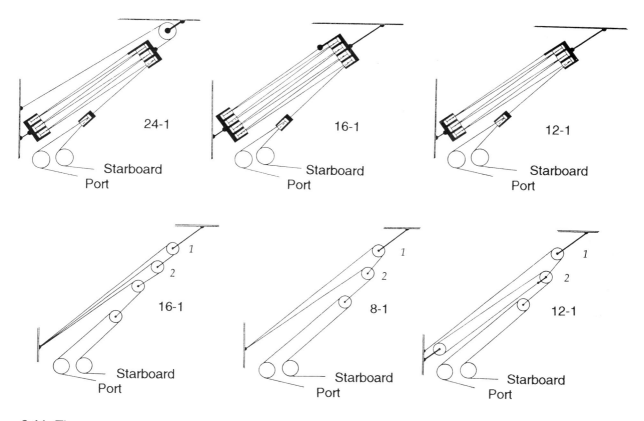

3.11: These are some examples of multi-block and cascade systems.

3.12: This strut on an International 14 uses a combination of a lever and a 2:1 block and tackle. The lever gives a reasonable amount of initial purchase simply and cheaply, and the addition of a couple of blocks allows you to double it.

3.13: A neat mast ram fitting on a 470. The length of the lever gives a 2:1 purchase, which is then increased by pulling it through the 4:1 rope purchase. The final mechanical advantage is given by multiplying the two together to give us 8:1.

Drums and Hydraulics

Although rare, you do occasionally see drums and hydraulics on racing dinghies. The drum provides a mechanical advantage that is dependant on the difference in diameter between the spindle and the drum (Illustration 3.14). The two most common uses for it are on the vang, or as a spinnaker halyard take-up. The drum vang is usually only seen, and rarely even then, on the Flying Dutchman. It is one of the few boats that has sufficient space at the bottom of the mast to fit the drum. Because the wider the drum the greater the purchase, you need a reasonable amount of room to make this system work. Another use is the spinnaker halyard take-up, where twisted elastic is used to drive a drum that reels up the slack in the spinnaker halyard. The drum increases the pulling power of the twisted elastic. On this occasion the transmission factor helps in taking up the rope - the wider the drum the more rope it will wind up per turn.

Hydraulics are a little more complex, using properties of fluid pressure to allow, as with pulleys and levers, a smaller force to move a larger load by travelling a greater distance (Illustration 3.15). Although at one time popular on yachts right down to 40 feet long, hydraulics have now been displaced by pulley and lever systems on all but the biggest Maxi yachts. Against that background it seems strange that they find their way on to dinghies, but there are

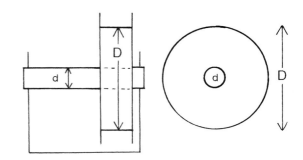

3.14: The drum provides a mechanical advantage by virtue of the difference in diameter between the spindle and the drum. The spindle is attached to the load, and the effort is applied to the drum. Then for each rotation the distance moved by the effort compared to the distance moved by the load is given by the ratio of the circumferences. Hence, Mechanical Advantage = $\pi D = \pi d$
$$MA = D/d$$

some efficient self-contained units that are useful on shrouds for instance. The advantage is in the space they take up, though personally we think a combination of pulleys and levers should always be lighter, more efficient and faster. And you can see much more easily when they are about to fail.

Because the Pressure P is constant in the system, then $\frac{f}{A} = \frac{F}{B}$, this is equation (i)

If area of cylinder piston (A) is $\frac{1}{4}$ of area of piston (B) $A = \frac{1}{4} B$

If we now substitute this into our equation (i) above, we have $f = \frac{F}{4}$

or that F is four times larger than f.

We can also show that if P is constant, then the volume of the hydraulic fluid is constant also. Then since;

Volume = area x distance moved by the piston and if B = 4A

It follows that if cylinder Piston A moves 1 inch then Piston B moves $\frac{1}{4}$ inch.

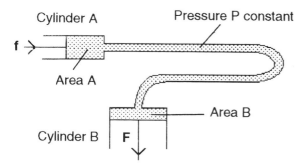

3.15: Hydraulics work by using the properties of fluids to enable a smaller force to move a larger load by travelling a greater distance:
Since Pressure $= \frac{Force}{Area}$ $P = \frac{f}{A}$ also $P = \frac{F}{B}$

Chapter 4

Choosing the Gear

When you come to fit a new system to your boat the final stage before getting out the tools will be choosing the fittings to do the job. By now you should have a list of all the bits you need. The number and type of blocks, cleats and fixing points. It pays to be as specific as you can about what you want at this stage, there is nothing worse than trekking miles to the nearest chandlery only to find you cannot remember what size shackle you need, or which way the block needs to lie and so what type of fixing you need. There are several considerations here, the first of which is the load the fitting will have to endure.

Loads

All the good equipment manufacturers provide the breaking loads of their fittings in their catalogue. This should enable you to choose the right fitting for the job, selecting the one with the breaking strain just above the load to which you expect it to be subjected. Which is all well and good - if you know the load that the fitting is going to have to handle.

This is the problem, the loadings that dinghy fittings are subjected to are not particularly well documented. Most fittings are selected on the basis of experience rather than measurement. Proper measurement would require the addition of load cells to the boat, complete with sampling, filtering and recording equipment. The problem is that the biggest loads are always dynamic, the ones that appear when you have just stopped the boat dead in the back of a wave after planing flat out in a huge gust. To find the actual peak load, which may last for only a fraction of a second, would take sophisticated measuring equipment that is not really suitable to the dinghy environment.

In the absence of this kind of work, we are left with the judgements of experience, and usually the people with the most of this are the equipment manufacturers and the chandlers.

As a first rule of thumb, shroud tensions in dinghies are usually at most 200kgs. So in rig systems the primary blocks must be designed with a working load of about 200kg. You should build into this a safety factor of about 4, ie. breaking loads on the first fitting in your rig tension system should be about 800kgs. This is also the approximate breaking strain on the most commonly used shroud wire. It is a good principle that each part of the system should fail at the same point. Although the weak link principle has its uses when one part of the system is a lot harder to fix than another. It may well be preferable for the vang to break rather than the boom for instance. So you could design the vang to fail at a load less than that which will break the boom. Although hardly a dinghy, this was the technique used on the 12 Metres at the 1987 *America*'s Cup in Fremantle. You can tie up the vang and carry on if it fails when you round the windward mark without releasing it - but you cannot sail on when the boom is in half.

Another way to think about it is the amount of physical strength it takes you to pull on the rope. A mainsheet load is unlikely to be more than about 50kg of steady pull at the tail. This means that if you have a 4:1 mainsheet system the load at the final boom attachment point will be about 200kgs. With a sheet you do not really need to build in much of a safety factor, as you will almost certainly be letting it go when things go wrong and the sail forces increase. A similar principle can be applied to the other systems, you work out about how hard you are going to be pulling on the rope. With a vang operating at 16:1 you are unlikely to use more than one hand on it - maybe 50kgs. But when it is really blowing, your 2:1 cunningham may well require pulling on as hard as you possibly can - perhaps 200kgs if you use your legs and arms jammed against the centreboard case! You can test these figures out for yourself in a gym, using a static rowing machine with a rope and pinned weights. Obviously it will vary enormously between your average 10,000 calories a day Star crew and a 60 kilo 470 helm. The problems arise after you cleat it, if it becomes subjected to big dynamic loads as the boat undergoes a disaster. The safety factor here should be between 2 to 4 depending on whether you think it is likely to undergo high dynamic loading, and whether it is the last thing you want to fail, or the first. Similarly there is no point having a 400kg rated block if you are going to screw it into a wooden thwart with a couple of self-tappers. Usually you will end up with a figure between two sizes of block - err on the side of safety, always choose the stronger fitting if you are not sure.

Weight

Which brings us to the next issue, the reason we are trying to pick the smallest fitting that will do the job - weight. 'Weight', as Uffa Fox memorably said, 'is only of use to steam rollers'. In the absence of any other parameters you should find the lightest fitting for the job. And this means comparing equipment from different materials and manufacturers. Often blocks that are the same size have dramatically different breaking loads. An example here is carbon blocks versus plastic ones. Often the same physical size of carbon block is slightly heavier, but it will cope with twice the load.

But it is not always the case that the lightest fitting is the one you want. Modern construction techniques often mean a boat can be built dramatically under the class minimum weight. If there is a limit to the amount of lead correctors you can put in, to bring it up to weight, you will need to fit the boat out as heavily as possible! Three-time World Fireball champion John Dransfield tells of his Delange boat that was so light it was fitted out with parts that were much stronger and heavier than those normally required. The result was a completely bombproof boat that in three years never broke anything and barely needed maintenance. John's devastating speed in a breeze was probably due in part to his complete confidence in the boat.

If you are fitting a boat out from scratch you should be conscious of the total weight right through the planning stage. If you possibly can you should weigh the bare hull, and then measure, or obtain from the brochures, the weight of all the fittings you intend to use. Add the two together, add a couple of kilos for the fastenings and see if it comes up to the class rule for the fitted out weight. If it is heavier, you either need lighter fittings, or you may need to go back to the system design stage and think out a lighter way of doing the job. If it is really overweight - give the boat back to the builder!!

If it is light, then you can start to think about where to add the weight. This is not always as obvious as it seems. Some classes require the correctors a long way forward in the boat. In the 470 for instance they must be up by the mast. It is worth going to some trouble to avoid having to add a couple of kilos there - you are better off with either the weight in the construction around the mast area, ie. the load bearing shroud points and triangulation, or in fittings further back in the boat. One theory has it that dinghies hinge off the transom when they pitch, rather than pivot around the centreboard. Next time you get the opportunity to watch your class going upwind in a breeze have a look at which point of the hull they are moving around - you may be surprised how far aft it is. Because of this it is becoming popular in the 470 not to worry too much about keeping the weight out of the back of the boat. What is for certain is that the back or middle is better than near or forward of the mast, the one place where you definitely do not need weight.

Cost

The unfortunate but inevitable factor of cost rears its ugly head once again. Even with ball bearing blocks commanding a premium of perhaps five times that of versions without, you can only afford not to use them when they do not make a difference to efficiency. And that usually means when there is not much load on the system. With only small loads, blocks without bearings run freely, with a significant load on they lock up. So for blocks, as for cleats. The harsh truth is, as we will see when we look at fitting design shortly, the more you spend, (assuming you do it intelligently), the better the boat will work.

Block Design

There are three basic designs of block; without bearings, with ball bearings and with needle bearings. In the first type the shive runs directly around the spindle. What this means is that when the block is loaded up the two surfaces of the spindle and the shive are pulled together. The surface area they run on increases and, because the two things are dependent, the friction increases and the block does not run freely. If you introduce ball bearings, they separate the two areas with the ball, which both reduces the contact area friction and of course rolls as well. But as the load increases further the balls will start to distort, flattening at the contact points - increasing the friction and decreasing their ability to roll. This can be avoided by using needle bearings, which because of their shape distort under a much higher load. The disadvantage is that they provide more contact area than ball bearings and so greater friction at lower loads. You can see this by spinning the sheaves of the different types of block. The ball bearing versions always run more freely - but you must remember how they will perform when under high load. This is why you will often find the blocks with the highest load specification use needle bearings.

Construction materials are the next consideration. Again it will depend on the load that the block is expected to undergo. The higher the load the more of it you are likely to find made from stainless steel. The various forms of plastic being the other main constituent. Carbon is just beginning to appear as a block material, and as the costs come down I think we can expect to see these blocks more widely used. They should provide more strength for less weight than either stainless steel or the plastics.

Any brief look at a chandlery's shelves will show you the variety of shapes and sizes that blocks come in; single, double or triples, with or without beckets, blocks for screwing down flat

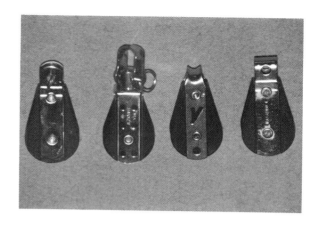

4.1: *Different block attachments, from the left; fork attachment, swivel attachment, simple loop attachment, loop/pin attachment.*

or suspending from ropes and so on. Be careful to choose the correct type of attachment on the block, so it is compatible to your fixing point. Blocks have to lie and swivel in the correct manner in order to work efficiently. Some of the different types of attachments on blocks are shown in illustration 4.1. There is the right shape of block for almost any imaginable use - almost. There will still be times when despite hours spent thumbing through the catalogues none of the manufacturers have yet latched on to your own individual design spec. Or if they have it will take three months to arrive from the factory in the Australian outback. One common example is the aft strop mainsheet system that uses the mainsheet itself to form the strop (Illustration 4.2 and see Chapter 6). The consequence of this is that the mainsheet is trying to split open the first block on the boom. In this case the block being used is double riveted but sometimes it is only a single rivet. Good preventative maintenance then demands the rivet be drilled out and a nut and bolt substituted.

For any kind of sheet, be it main, jib or spinnaker, one of the most useful pieces of equipment is the ratchet block. These are ball bearing blocks that only rotate one way - as you pull the sheet in. As you ease it the shive locks against an internal ratchet, the serrated surface then provides additional friction for the rope on

4.2: The aft mainsheet strop system on a Fireball. Note how the block is attached here - there is a u-bolt through the top edge of the boom to spread the load and get the attachment point as high up as possible. It also straddles the mainsail track to get it out to the furthest point on the boom. This in turn is cut to minimum length to save on weight - extra length here only helps to trip up the boat when the boom end catches the water.

4.3: The ratchet block works by only turning in one direction - to pull the rope in. The serrations then provide grip to make it easier to hold the sheet against the load.

the shive (Illustration 4.3). It is a lot easier on your arms, but a lot tougher on the sheets. They also make it easier to unjam the sheet, sometimes in a gust you cannot get the sheet out of the cleat to ease it - the ratchet takes sufficient load off to solve this problem. But there is a difficulty with the wind dropping and you not being able to ease the sheet against all the friction that is so useful in a breeze. Which is why the dual-use blocks are now so popular, with a facility to click the ratchet on and off. In light airs the block runs freely in both directions, in a breeze it locks as you ease the sheet. Apart from the additional weight these blocks involve, and the cost, there are few potential disadvantages. British Olympic 470 crew Andy Hemmings pointed out one - that it is possible to drop the sheet into the cleat without noticing when using a ratchet - because there is not much load on it anyway. And we all know what happens when you tack a dinghy with the jib sheet cleated! But for the most part they are a plus, crews will be able to work the kite harder downwind, and in a breeze it becomes a lot easier to play the jib properly rather than jamming it. The macho 'I'm too tough to need a ratchet' attitude also seems to have disappeared, crews realising that anything that increases their effective work rate is fast.

Cleats

The second type of fitting that we find everywhere on the boat is the cleat, in all its various forms. First up is the Clam cleat (Illustration 4.4) which, because it has no moving parts, is particularly reliable. The only thing you have to watch out for is the grooves wearing. This happens a lot quicker on the plastic versions than the aluminium ones and we would only advise their use on light, low importance ropes. This type of cleat generally is best used for ropes that do not have to be let off too quickly, or in an emergency. Because the harder the rope pulls on them, the harder the cleat bites, they are not suitable for sheets or the vang. When you want to release them quickly and easily, they are most under load and therefore hardest to get out. But something

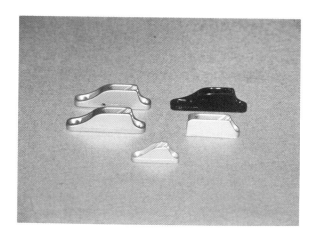

4.4: *Some of the Clam cleat family, patented and trademarked to one company.*

4.6: *Cam cleats from various manufacturers. These are the best solution for any rope that has a high load, needs careful adjustment or may need to be released in a hurry.*

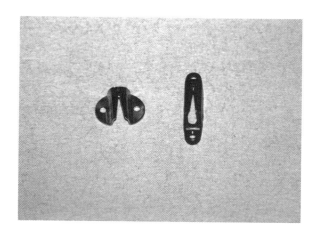

4.5: *A couple of V-cleats, a simplified version of the Clam cleat. Because it holds the rope in just one place it is more prone to failure and wear, as well as being harder to release under load.*

like the cunningham or outhaul, which rarely if ever is released in an emergency, is an ideal use. The other disadvantage to these cleats is their lack of positive grip on a rope that has little or no load on it. You have to push the rope into the cleat to get it to grip - all of which takes a little more time. Note also that the diameter of rope should be carefully matched to the cleat. The V-cleat (Illustration 4.5) is a more basic version of the Clam cleat. It is not as reliable, because there is only one gripping V, and consequently it is also more likely to

damage the rope. Not recommended for much except low load, low importance uses.

For sheets and the vang tail you need cam cleats (Illustration 4.6). Because they have moving parts these can be less reliable if they are not looked after - salt washed off them and so on. But they are essential for sheets because they provide an even, positive grip on the rope whatever the load - you should always be able to release them. The better quality cam cleats have some form of bearing which allows you to drop the rope into the cleat rather than pull it through and in. An important point when you are trying to trim a jib to within millimetres. But the real trick to the design of these fittings is the design of the cams themselves, it has to be just right so that the rope will come out easily under load, but not fly out of its own accord. The angle of the cleat to the load is important, the rope should always be pulled down into the cleat. Most manufacturers make wedges to fit under the cleats so you can vary the angle they operate at. If you have problems with the wedged cleat releasing itself you should check that the cantilever load on the bolts has not altered the cleat's angle (see Chapter 1). If not, and the cam design appears to allow the sheet to release of its own accord, there is a way round it, other than changing the cleat. What you do is file tiny grooves across the serrations

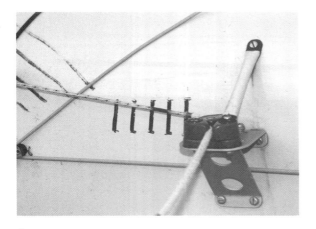

a

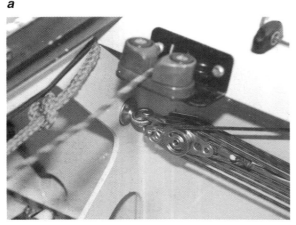

b

c

in the cam, this just gives it a bit more grip on the rope when it tries to slip upwards and out of the cleat. The cleat mounting is important to enable it to be operated in the most efficient manner, sometimes this will mean making up a bracket (Illustration 4.7).

Another important variation is the pump cleat, which automatically allows the rope to pass freely one way, whilst jamming it the other (Illustration 4.8). The normal use for this is on pump action spinnaker systems (see Chapter 8), but we are confident that someone, somewhere, has found an alternative use for it. They are simple and generally reliable. Though we are not personal fans of pump spinnaker halyard systems, the cleat failing is not usually the problem.

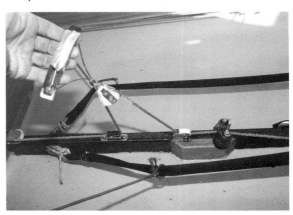

4.8: *The pump cleat (black with Northfix name) which works by pivoting on an off-centre point, so that as the rope goes through one way it is pulled into line and so allows it through, but as it tries to reverse the cleat tilts and so jams.*

4.7: *Various brackets constructed for cam cleats; (a) is a jib sheet turning block and cleat mounting on a 470, (b) is the vang exiting from the centreboard capping on a 470, (c) is the same as seen on an International 14.*

Part Two

Chapter 5
Mast Control Systems

We have already discussed in Chapter 2 the overall techniques for controlling the mast, and how to arrive at a general system design. Here we will consider how to make it happen.

Mast Ram

Under the heading mast ram we will include all the possible means of controlling mast bend by applying force at or below the goose neck, so it includes struts and levers as well as rams.

First up and the simplest method is chocking the mast gate (Illustration 5.1). This is all that is allowed in classes like the 420, and despite its simplicity it is still reasonably efficient - so long as you do not want to alter it too often! Wood is probably the best material for the chocks. Plastics are a little too slippery and tend to slide out under load. But wood will need to be quite carefully shaped to fit the gate otherwise it will crack. A set of chocks, each about five millimetres thick, is the best idea - you can confuse yourself too easily with different

thicknesses. The 420's bigger brother, the 470, has a popular variation on this theme, shown in illustration 5.2. The swatcher is simple and cheap but difficult to adjust under load. If you are going to use this you will probably be unable to adjust the mast upwind. But it has the benefit of being precise, so you always know exactly how much ram you have on.

5.1: Simple wooden mast chocks on a 420.

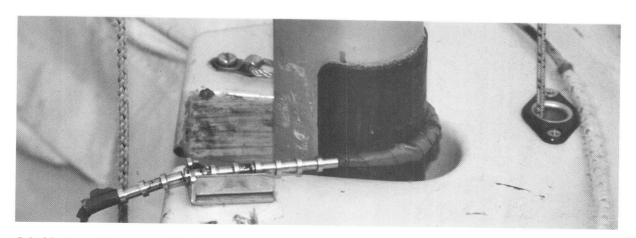

5.2: Mast swatcher on a 470, the mast position is altered by the number of stainless tube chocks positioned behind the small gate fitting.

Now we come onto what are more precisely called mast rams, devices that push the mast backwards. They can be powered in a multitude of ways. The one shown in illustration 5.3 uses a mighty screw. Rotating the large radius wheel with the rope system shown spins the rod in the thread and extends the ram against the mast. The big advantage this does have compared to the two systems above, is that it holds the mast completely firm - it cannot move either forwards or backwards. Consequently it will induce more bend in the mast as well as restrict it. It is also the first system that we have shown that could be operated from a distance. A rope can be led aft to either the helmsman or the crew. Not a particularly easy job, because it must form a continuous tensioned loop to work on the screw - but possible. If controlling the ram from a distance is your priority there are better ways of achieving it.

One way is with a system like that shown in illustration 3.13, where both the lever and the block and tackle contribute to the purchase (see Chapter 3). Although it has not been done

5.3: The mighty screw used as a mast ram. This device obtains its mechanical advantage in exactly the same way as the drum (see Chapter 3). The rope around the serrated large radius wheel turns the screw in the thread, moving the mast forwards or backwards.

because of the 470 class rules, this system is easily controlled from a distance. One end of the purchase can be led aft to the crew or helmsman on either side. It is also mechanically efficient, the only friction involved is a little in the blocks and in the pivot point of the lever. You should be able to pull the mast back one-handed even with the vang still on. But you need to keep a careful track of the rope markings to know where the mast is in the gate. A combination of marking both the gate and the rope is a good idea, as rope stretch can be periodically checked against the more positive gate markings. The disadvantages are that it is complicated to make it work both ways, ie. to push and pull the mast you need two purchase systems. Secondly, because the end of the levers movement describes a circle rather than a straight line, its operating distance is limited. This need not be a problem but it can require careful setting up.

Levers can also be used to provide the power to the next type of mast control - the strut. These differ from rams in that they operate higher up the mast, closer to the goose neck, and therefore more directly oppose the forward bending component of the boom (Illustration 5.4). Struts can also be powered by placing the other end on a track. The track needs to be low friction, otherwise this system is hard to use. It is a lot more compact than the lever, requiring less space to fit, but it has the same disadvantage of requiring two purchase systems to drive the mast both ways (Illustration 5.5).

The final possibility is lowers, wires attached to the mast at goose neck height and taken back to the shroud base area (Illustration 5.6). Because they are wire they can only pull the mast back and not push it forward. The advantage over a strut is that they also support the mast sideways. So when the boom is eased on a reach the lowers oppose its bending component on the mast. The result is a straighter mast, tighter leech and more power from the rig. Multi-block, lever or cascade systems can all be used to pull them on.

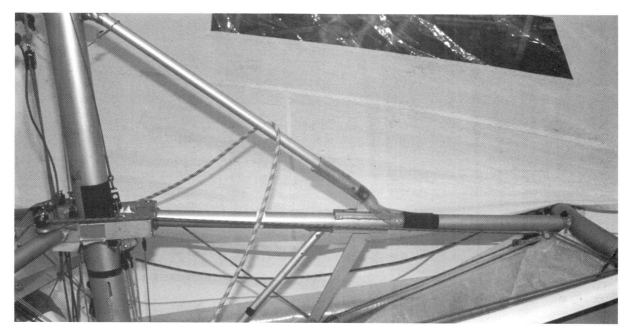

5.4: *The mast strut powered by a lever. The two rope purchase systems, one at 1:1 the other at 2:1, pull it either forwards or backwards. In this way it opposes or increases the amount of bend at goose neck level - directly opposing the thrust from the boom.*

5.5: *Another version of the strut, this time powered by one end running on a track. The track can be placed on the deck and run horizontally as well as the vertical system shown here. The wire attached to the car on the track runs off to a multi-block purchase system below deck level. Notice that there is only one purchase system on the car, so this strut can only restrict mast bend and not induce it. Although the track has been drilled out so that a pin can be used to induce pre-bend (if the mast is pushed forward by hand) or restrict the amount of ram applied. This would stop you inverting the mast accidentally.*

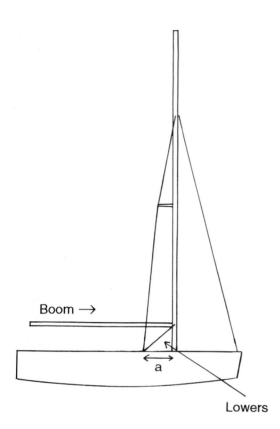

Boom →

a

Lowers

5.6: The lowers run from goose neck height to the shroud base area and restrict mast bend forwards and sideways. The bigger 'a' is, the more effective they are fore and aft, and the less effective sideways.

Spreader Systems: Fore and Aft

Spreader adjustment is one of those things you either love or you hate. Some people bolt and ignore them, others can hardly stop themselves fiddling with them. At least part of the urge to bolt them derives from the fact that there are few completely satisfactory methods of adjusting them - certainly not while you are sailing. The best that can usually be achieved is that you stop sailing and alter them whilst standing on the foredeck. The systems that allow this inevitably work on a threaded screw principle.

The most common is the one seen in illustration 5.7, the wing adjuster. Which is basically a bolt that threads through the end of the spreader to butt up against the forward

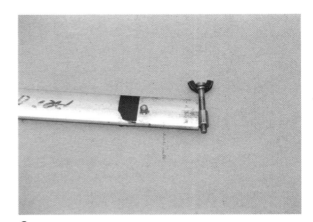

a

b

5.7: Wing nut spreader adjusters, seen on the end of the spreader in (a), and in position in (b). Notice the reminder on which way to turn the screw painted on the mast, and the wire loop to stop the spreader popping out backwards. The red elastic looped round the wing nut is to stop them turning on their own, particularly when the load is off the spreader, as when trailing the boat for instance. Nevertheless you should always re-calibrate the spreader adjustment when you rig the boat - for instance, so many turns on from a known base point.

inside face of the spreader bracket. Wind it in and it pushes the outboard end of the spreader forward, wind it out and the outboard end moves aft. It is simple and relatively foolproof, but there are a couple of essential tweaks for trouble free operation. The first is to ensure that the face of the spreader bracket that the bolt works against is perpendicular to the bolt.

Otherwise the load will bend the bolt and you will not be able to wind it back out. This usually means some work on the inside of the spreader bracket, some mast makers produce a special chock that can be glued in place, with others you will need to pack it with Coke can and glue.

Secondly, because the spreader is free pivoting there is a real danger, especially on spinnaker boats, that the mast will be allowed to invert, ie pop out backwards. To avoid this you need to drill through at the aft end of the bracket and put a bolt through to limit the movement of the spreader. If there is no room for this it is also possible to drill through both the bracket and the spreader, and then use a much smaller diameter bolt which allows the spreader some movement. But you need to get the spreader on its average position before you do this, otherwise you will end up with the two holes too far apart to get a strong enough bolt through. It also pays with these systems to tape or elasticate the adjusters in place. Otherwise they can spin off a half turn when you are trailing or they are not under load, and ruin your carefully set-up boat tune.

One of the mast manufacturers makes a version on the same theme (Illustration 5.8) which are simpler to set up, requiring none of the time consuming tweaks described above. They hold the spreader in both directions, and are nearly as easy to adjust. Another proprietary system is seen in illustration 5.9, where the variety of bolt holes is intended to provide sufficient adjustment. But sometimes this is simply not fine enough, it can be frustrating if the spreader position you want is between two holes. But it does have the advantage of holding the spreader firmly in both directions. However, it is almost impossible to adjust spreaders on the water with this system.

The systems we have covered so far will cope with the majority of classes. Other solutions are possible, some of which appear in the International Moth class. We have shown one in illustration 5.10, which uses fixed spreaders and varies the point of adjustment onto the mast bracket.

a

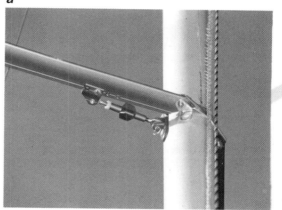

b

5.8: *Two versions of a proprietary spreader adjustment, both dispense with many of the problems and necessary tweaks with the wing nut version, but on (a) adjustment is provided by the inboard end being detached and the tube threaded to the new position before being reattached - which is considerably less convenient to use. Whereas (b) is adjustable just by turning the gnarled section.*

5.9: *Another version on the spreader angle theme, the sets of bolt holes providing the adjustment.*

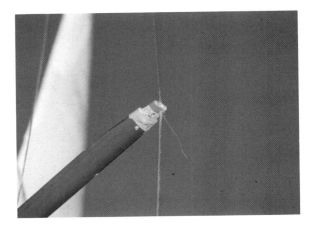

5.11: Spreader length adjustment provided by the attachment to the shroud being inserted into the main part of the spreader. It can then be moved in or out on a set of pin holes.

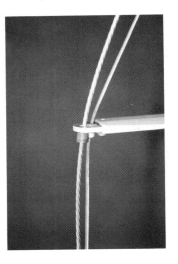

5.10: International Moth spreader system, with adjustment provided by moving the point of attachment to the mast fore and aft on a rack and pin system.

5.12: A ferrule fixed onto a shroud to limit the vertical movement of the spreader on the wire.

Spreader Systems: Length

Adjustment of spreader length is often a much lower priority than the fore and aft position. So the available systems tend to restrict adjustment to off the water - if adjustment is available at all. Some systems just allow you to cut the spreader to length and fix it at the outboard end. Others provide adjustment, usually in a fashion like that in illustration 5.11. Care does need to be exercised with these though, if the adjuster is extended too far and a lot of rig tension is being used then they can collapse. A further tweak, seen in illustration 5.12 is to limit the movement of the outboard end of the spreader up and down the shroud. This keeps it in the right position (with equal angles between spreader and shroud, top and bottom) and reduces the chance of the loads becoming unbalanced and the spreader collapsing.

5.13: The simplest method of adjusting jib halyard tension - loop it onto a variable hook up rack. But with any amount of rig tension it becomes almost impossible to adjust on the water, you need someone hanging on the forestay to get the loop onto the rack.

Rig Tension and Mast Rake Control Systems

There are three methods of adjusting the rig tension and mast rake. You can fix the shrouds and adjust the jib halyard, or fix the jib halyard and adjust the shrouds - or adjust both. Because the jib halyard has a significant effect on the mast bend as well as the rake, this last method is the best. But remember that with a hog stepped mast if you change the shroud

a

b

5.14: 470 jib halyard tension system, with the halyard exiting the base of the mast (a) and hooking onto an 8:1 block and tackle (b).

positions up or down and pull on the same jib tension you will still alter the mast bend - because the spreaders have not been adjusted (see Chapter 2). Of course that may be what you want, but it is also off track and onto boat tune issues, so we will move on to the methods of adjusting the jib halyard.

The simplest method is to bring the tail of the halyard, in the form of a loop, out of the side of the mast and hook it up onto a rack. This is the only system allowed in the 420 class, and it requires a gorilla, or at least a heavy man, dangling on the forestay to get any worthwhile amount of rig tension on (Illustration 5.13). The most common method is to bring a loop out of the base or side of the mast and hook it up to a

43

purchase system. This could be a lever or a muscle box, but in recent years has tended to be an 8:1 or above block and tackle. Because these can be constructed with a lot more throw than either a lever or muscle box, it enables you to hook the halyard on and wind the tension up without your gorilla hanging on the forestay. And, because you can slack the system right off this has a couple of other benefits; firstly, on boats like the 470 that only have pinned shroud adjustment, it enables you to alter the rake on the water.It also has the consequence of allowing you to get the jib down in an emergency.The 470 system shown in illustration 5.14 is typical. This system, or variations on it, are hard to beat.

The other possible complication is the use of a 2:1 at the hounds (Illustration 5.15). This entails fixing one end of the halyard at the hounds, running it through a block which is shackled to the head of the jib, and then into the sheave and down the mast. The advantage of this system, though it takes some serious maths to establish it, is that it reduces compression on the mast. The disadvantage is that the wire splice at the loose tail of the halyard may not go out through the sheave at the hounds. So you can end up shackling the jib on standing on the foredeck. Not a big problem unless you have got the kind of foredeck that a tantrum throwing two year-old could stamp their foot through. It is sometimes possible to file down the back of the jib halyard box to allow the splice through - worth checking if you use this system. Because the wire is under less load you can also use lighter wire, perhaps 3mm rather than 3.5mm.

Adjustable shrouds can be one of the most complicated items to set up, they can also be one of the simplest, it really depends on the amount of adjustment you need. In its most straightforward form the shrouds will just pin

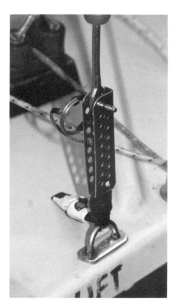

5.15: A 2:1 on the jib halyard before it enters into the mast. The halyard runs from a fixed point through a block on the top of the jib wire and then into the mast and down to a normal halyard exit.

5.16: Shroud adjustment as seen on the 470, it being pinned into different positions on the rack.

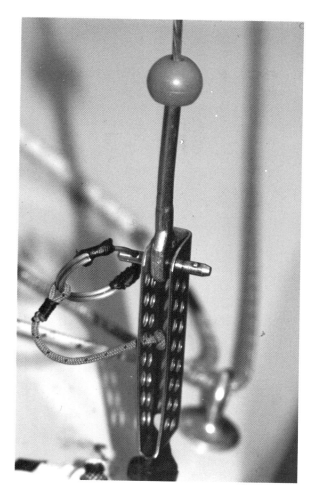

5.17: *The same adjuster as 5.16, with detail of the fast pin. These use a tiny sprung ball to keep the pin in place - much quicker than a clevis pin with a split ring. Note the string keeping it attached to the boat, and the bobble ferruled in place on the shroud. This makes it easier to force the shroud into the right place on the adjuster with cold, wet hands.*

5.18: *Staymaster shroud adjuster, the clip around the nut drops down to allow you to turn the nut. This threads the serrated plate on the end of the shroud down between the two plates fixed to the boat's shroud base. The numbers on the serrated plate are used for the calibration.*

into an adjustable rack (Illustration 5.16). The big disadvantage is of course that you have to detach the shroud to change the rake - not the kind of thing that you are likely to tackle up the first beat. Nevertheless this is the kind of set-up that the 470's are forced to use by the class rules and they are adept at changing it between races, even in 30 knots of breeze. The technique is to put the boat on a close reach, then drop off the rig tension completely and pull

on the vang to bring the rig back as far as possible. This should, if you have enough throw in the jib tension system, slacken off the leeward shroud enabling you to alter it. Fast-pins are almost as useful as they are expensive at this point, and if they are tied on to the boat it prevents the embarrassment of dropping either the pin or the split ring (Illustration 5.17). Once altered you let the vang go, pull the rig upright enough to tack the boat and repeat it for the other side.

The next stage up is the Staymaster (Illustration 5.18) which although it still cannot be adjusted without easing the rig tension at least does not require the complete detachment of the shroud. There are also shroud levers (Illustration 3.6), which combine a rack and pin system to give you the kind of fine adjustment you need to make to tune the rake upwind, with a lever to allow you to let the whole rig go forward downwind - but watch your fingers when letting it off in a breeze.

If you want real adjustment though, you need to run the shroud onto some kind of purchase system, and this is where it gets complicated. The problem is not about applying adequate force to the shroud, but in doing so accurately and evenly to both sides. The basic techniques are either the straightforward block and tackle (Illustration 5.19) or a lever, maybe combined with a block and tackle (Illustration 5.20). In some hulls it will be easier to get the blocks to lead cleanly than on others. The FD is a particularly good example as it has the whole gunwale to hide the purchase system under. The International 14 and 505 are both quite a bit harder to arrange as we can see from the illustrations (5.19/20). Whether you try to link the two shrouds together or not, you must be careful about the calibration of the system - sailing with one shroud shorter or longer than the other is not fast.

a

5.19: *Shroud adjustment on a 505, the initial 2:1 on the shroud (a) is run through the side tank and attached to a 7:1 multi-block system (b). The tail from each shroud being connected together (c) so that both the shrouds can be adjusted at the same time with an additional 2:1 purchase. Note the calibration check strips in (b).*

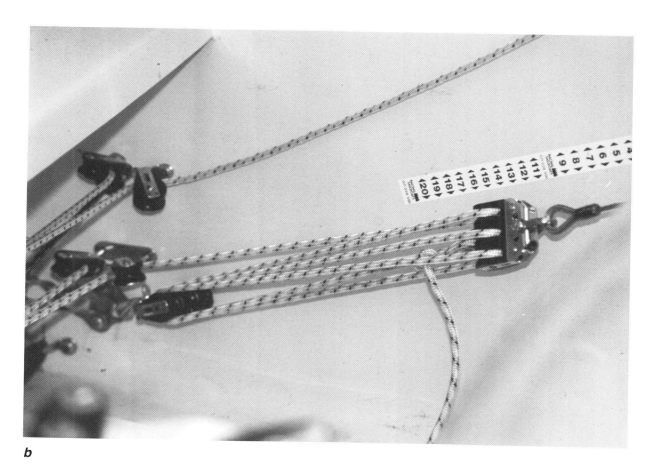

b

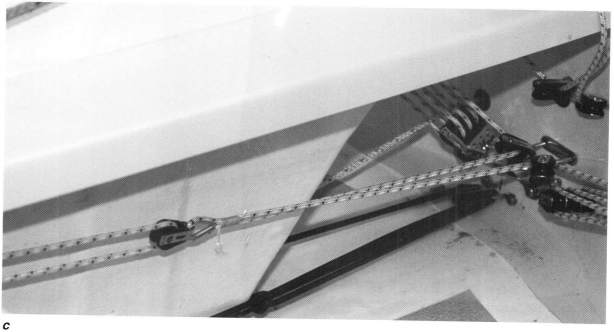

c

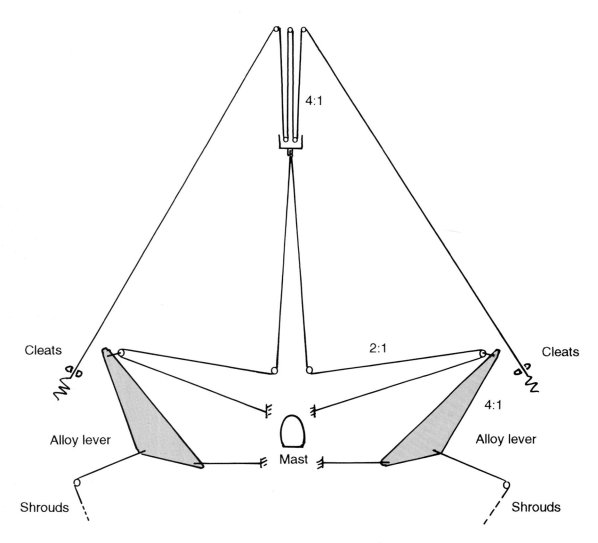

5.20: *A popular shroud adjustment system for the International 14. The shrouds are linked through turning blocks direct to a 4:1 lever each side. This is adjusted with a 2:1 purchase, linked onto a 4:1 multi-block system. This gives a total of 32:1.*

There are a couple of other lesser used options, one is hydraulics. But since the whole of the keelboat world has been trying to get these off racing boats for the last ten years putting them on a dinghy seems a bit perverse. A simple block and tackle solution that is easier to set up than either of the two above, but is neither as efficient nor as adjustable, is to put a muscle box on the end of each shroud (Illustration 5.21). The other possibility, which is a lot more interesting, is putting the heel of the mast on a ramped track, as we see in illustration 5.22. With this system the entire mast heel can be hauled up a track with the muscle box. The idea is to get the angle of the track such that the rig tension stays constant as the mast heel is moved forward or aft. The mast is then pivoting around the hounds, with the rake altering as the mast foot moves.

5.21: A simple solution to shroud adjustability - a muscle box on each one. We have already commented on the inefficiency of muscle boxes. And because the shrouds are adjusted separately you must be careful to maintain them at an even length.

5.22: The muscle box just forward of the mast is used to pull the mast foot up a ramped track (hidden by the wood centreboard case). The intention is to maintain the same rig tension whilst moving the mast foot and hence changing the rake. Strictly speaking you should use a curved track - but that is a major engineering problem.

Chapter 6

Mainsail Systems

Mainsail control systems include the vang, cunningham and outhaul, but most important is the sheeting system. Although at first glance the method you choose to do this job is just another way of pulling the sail in, in fact it plays a large part in determining how you sail the boat.

Mainsheet Systems

The important factors to consider here are how the sheeting arrangement will trim the sail, how easy it is to tack, gybe and sheet in and out, and how simple, light and reliable you can keep it. None of the systems score heavily on all three points, and which one you place the emphasis on says a lot about your approach to sailing the boat. Generally you can apply the load to the mainsail from one of two places, the middle or the end of the boom. If you use the end, you have more leverage on the leech for the same force on the sheet. This is because you are pulling down on it from a greater

distance from its pivot (the goose neck), than with a centre mainsheet.

The final take-off point, which you hang on to the sheet from, can also come from the middle of the boat or the transom. The centre mainsheet means tacking and gybing facing forwards with the tiller behind you and the mainsheet in front. The aft mainsheet means tacking facing backwards with both sheet and tiller coming at you from the same direction, but you cannot see where the bow of the boat is. The other problem with the mainsheet lead coming from the transom is that it pulls you towards the back of the boat when there is any amount of breeze. The resulting position, with legs wrapped around thwarts to keep you in place and the body twisted to control the sheet, is highly unergonomic. As a consequence we have seen the development of systems that, although attached to the boom at the transom, are then led forward, either through or under the boom, to a centre mainsheet take-off point (Illustration 6.1).

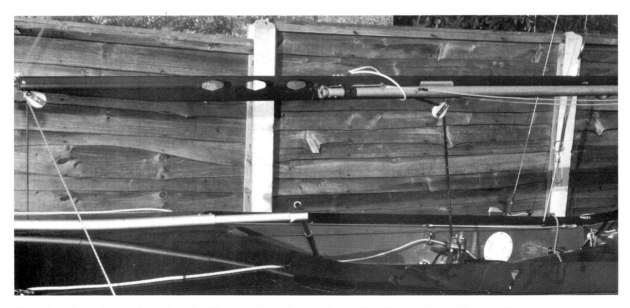

6.1: An aft mainsheet system led forward to a take-off point in the centre of the boat.

6.2: *The aft mainsheet in its simplest form, we can see the awkwardness of sailing with the sheet leading from the transom.*

6.3a

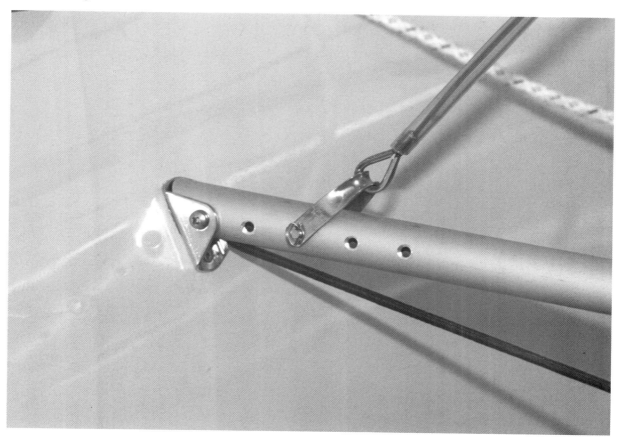

b

6.3: *The 420 mainsheet system showing (a) the strops running up from the traveller bar to the purchase system at the top, and (b) the limited adjustment of the strop length.*

There are some classes which still insist on the aft mainsheet as part of their class rules. The Enterprise is one, and in illustration 6.2 we can see the aft mainsheet in its most basic form. Apart from the awkwardness of the aft sheet lead, which we have already mentioned, the other aspect is an inability to get the boom on the centreline (Though this does not seem to be a problem for the Enterprise class, where no effort is made to overcome it. However, it would be deficient if applied to the 470 for instance, where the main does need to be centred). However hard you pull you can never get the boom directly above the take-off point on the centreline. This is at its worst in light to medium airs when you need the mainsheet on the centreline with moderate leech tension. But the harder you pull to get it on the centreline the more excessive the leech tension you apply - the sheeting system is causing the two things you are trying to achieve to work against each other so you have neither. You could centre the main by putting the fixed point on the transom on a traveller track and pulling it to windward. But that makes it considerably harder to tack. Overall this system scores badly on its ability to trim the sail accurately, and it is hard to play the sheet. However, it is easy to tack (unless you install a traveller) and gybe, and is light and simple to fit.

Similarly limited is the basic 420 centre mainsheet system in illustration 6.3. Again it is both simple to fit and easy to use - once you have the knack of tacking facing forwards - but it is impossible to centre the mainsheet. At exactly the opposite end of the spectrum is the centre mainsheet with a traveller (Illustration 6.4). This puts the mainsheet take-off point on a car mounted on a lateral track. The traveller car can be pulled across the boat from either side, allowing you to drag the mainsail onto the centreline when going to windward.

6.4: *Mainsheet traveller system on a Merlin Rocket. The black rope running through the traveller car drags it to starboard, and the white one pulls it to port.*

The traveller allows for the complete range of trim, because the boom can be moved laterally across the boat independently of the amount of sheet and leech tension applied. This is its strongest aspect, where it falls down is in weight, complexity and ease of sailing. Straight-lining is not too bad, although you have to play both the sheet and traveller to keep the sail at 100% through gusty conditions. But it is awkward when you want to move fore and aft in the boat. Gybing is straightforward, it is tacking, when the traveller has to be adjusted through the manoeuvre, that takes some practice. The worst scenario is forgetting to uncleat the windward side into the tack. After you are round it is now the leeward side, and you cannot pull the traveller up to its new position without going down to leeward to uncleat it.

Of course such skills can be learned, but if your attitude is that the boat should sail itself whilst you get on with the race you might be looking for something a little simpler. One solution has been to devise some clever fittings to help. The best, and the most expensive, are the type of twin cleats that unjam to leeward as you pull them up to windward (Illustration 6.5). But whilst this makes it easier to sail, it adds more complex fittings, hence more weight and reliability risk. A simpler solution is the strop system (Illustration 6.6). These trade off some of the sheeting flexibility of the traveller system for greater simplicity in both fitting and sailing. They allow you to tack the boat without adjusting anything more than the mainsheet. But to get the trim right you must have the right strop height, as we can see from illustration 6.6 (b) and (c). If they are too short or long you are worse off than with an aft mainsheet, in terms of getting the main on the centreline. This is particularly important when you consider that as you rake, the boom moves up and down. So you need to be able to adjust the strop height along with the rake. In fact, even with the strops set correctly you will still not quite get the boom centred - but this is the loss you accept for an easier to use system. It is possible to centre the main if you adjust the strops with each tack (Illustration 6.6 (d)). Then it is equivalent to the traveller in terms of sail trim and ease of use, but considerably lighter because you have dispensed with the track. The downside of the strops is having them flap around in the bottom of the boat during tacks, gybes and slow speed manoeuvring.

6.5: *This traveller car uncleats the leeward control line when you pull on the windward one.*

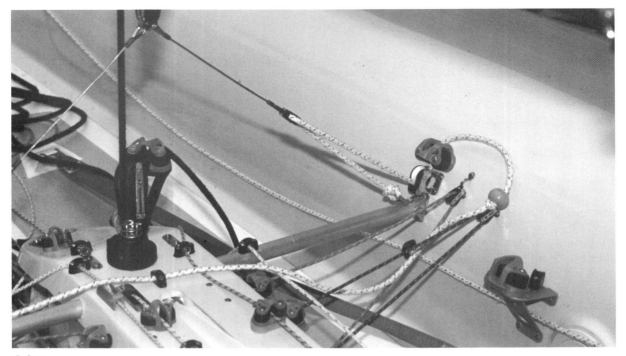

6.6a

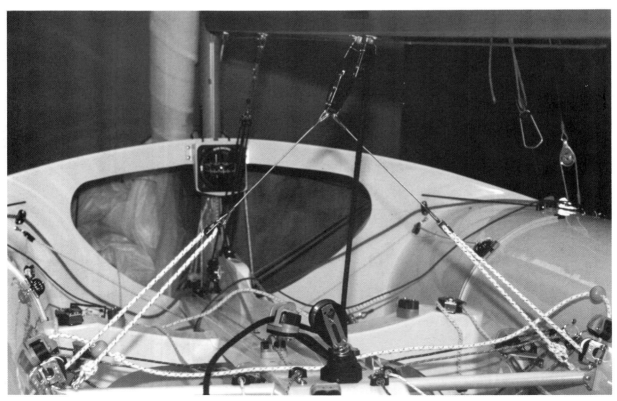

6.6b

54

6.6: Adjustable strops on a 505 mainsheet, (a) the effective take-off point that the mainsail is sheeted from can be moved up and down with the strop height, which has the same effect as moving it to windward. But in (b) and (c) we can see that even though the strop height is set up correctly for the rake (so that the sheet can go block to block) the mainsail is still not on the centreline. This can be overcome by pulling the windward strop tighter to pull the sheeting take-off point to windward - as you would with a traveller. You then have the same problem of having to adjust them through a tack. (d) shows that by attaching a line (of exactly the right length) to the two strops just before they go into the jammer, when the windward strop is pulled tight the leeward one is pulled out of the cleat. In other words the line is fractionally too short to allow them both to be cleated at the same time. The same principle as the traveller car in 6.5.

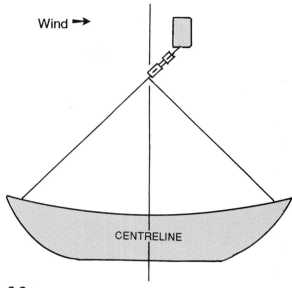

6.6c

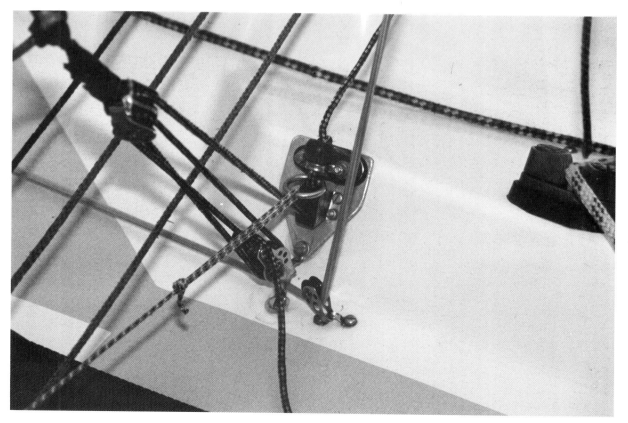

6.6d

55

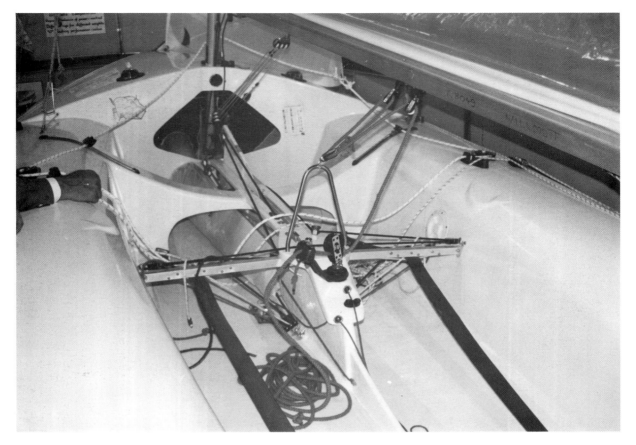

6.7: *A fixed hoop seen on a 505 - the big disadvantage is that you cannot adjust the height as you can with adjustable strops.*

A variation on this theme is the hoop, which gets round this problem, being essentially a solid strop (Illustration 6.7). It also makes the boat a lot easier to move around in, especially fore and aft, as it has a narrower base. The disadvantage is that being solid it is harder to adjust the height. There are two ways of doing it. The first is to move the whole hoop to windward each time to keep the boom on the centreline. But the advantages over a traveller are minimal, since you have to adjust it with each tack - not as far, but far enough - and there is nearly as much hardware involved. Another solution, as seen in illustration 6.8, is to be able to adjust the take-off point on the top of the hoop in a vertical plane. This can also be done with a sprung pin. The other advantage of the hoop is that it gives you something to pull yourself across the boat on when roll-tacking!

But the vertically adjusted hoop will not centre the main, so although they are simpler to sail with than a traveller, by now there is nearly as much equipment in the boat and we do not have the traveller's flexibility in sail trim. One system that will provide it is the strut, as seen in illustration 6.9. This is a laterally pivoting bar whose top can be pulled to windward from either side. It gives you the same ability as the traveller does, to sheet the boom on the centreline. Whether it does it with any gain in ease of use is a matter of conjecture. You still have to adjust the system after every tack. There is a little less equipment, no heavy metal track across the boat, but it is as limiting to your manoeuvrability around the boat as the strops. Another compilation system is the square

56

6.8a

6.8 a & b: Two methods of adjusting the height of a hoop seen on 470's, allowing the take-off point to move vertically whilst the hoop provides lateral support.

6.8b

6.9: A strut used on an International 14, the 2:1 attached to the top of the strut is used to pull it to windward and so centre the mainsail.

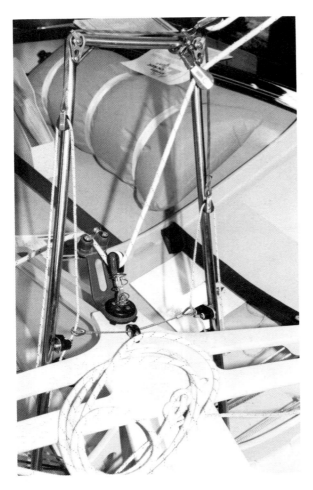

6.10: The square topped hoop, which allows you to pull the mainsheet take-off point along the top. You do not need to pull it so far to centre the mainsail as with a traveller, and this one incorporates a wire loop to uncleat the leeward side each time you tack. This is the same principle as on the adjustable strops in 6.6(d).

topped hoop, where you can pull the mainsheet take-off point to windward along the top of the hoop. Again the advantages over the traveller are limited. It gives you the same flexibility of sail trim and less restriction on crew movement fore and aft. It is a little easier to tack because you do not have to pull the mainsheet car so far. And you can get the leeward side to uncleat automatically without the cost of the special traveller car. But it is a lot of hardware -

meaning weight and potential failures (Illustration 6.10).

The final system is both one of the simplest, and provides the trimming ability of the traveller. It is the split sheet, aft to centre system, as seen in illustration 6.11. The mainsheet itself forms the strops for an aft mainsheet, that is then run forward along the boom to a centre main take-off point. The strop length needs to be carefully set-up initially. But provided that when the mast is at its most upright the two parts of the sheet enter the boom block it will still work as you rake. The key to it is that when the two parts of the sheet/strop run into the boom it must be centred - by necessity of being pulled under equal tension from the two corners of the boat. Any further tension on the sheet simply loads the leech up directly.

By using the sheet and the vang together you will achieve any trim that a traveller can, and still tack the boat without having to adjust anything. The system is also simple, requiring only a standard 3:1 centre main take-off in the middle of the boat. The disadvantages, and there had to be some, are twofold, firstly in the amount of rope that you need. This makes it difficult to trim in quickly when two-sail reaching, ducking another boat or rounding marks. It also sits in the bottom of the boat sucking up water and adding weight - though modern fibre technology means this last can be (expensively) avoided by use of composite sheets. Spectra is used in the section that bears the load upwind and close reaching, then polypropylene is used in the rest of the tail - neither of these fibres absorb water. The final problem is gybing, the slack mainsheet is inclined to trap itself under the gunwale at the transom - inconvenient but not usually disastrous.

One final comment; for every system here, bar one, easing the sheet in a gust releases the leech. With a traveller you can let the boom down on the traveller car, whilst keeping the sheet, and hence the leech, jammed. But all the other systems rely on easing the sheet to drop the boom to leeward, and consequently lose control of the leech. To avoid this you need a powerful and efficient vang - our next topic.

6.11: The split aft mainsheet, which centres the sail automatically, (a) and (b). This is because as the two parts go through the block (c) it guarantees that the boom is under equal tension from both sides. The mainsheet is led forward inside the boom and emerges through a slot cut in the underside (d) just before the final boom take-off block. In (e), next page, we can see the mainsheet running forward externally in a sailcloth protector. This is to stop the mainsheet looping itself round your head when you tack or gybe. Running it externally saves cutting the weakening exit hole for the sheet in the middle of the boom.

c

a

d

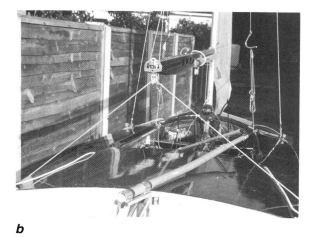

b

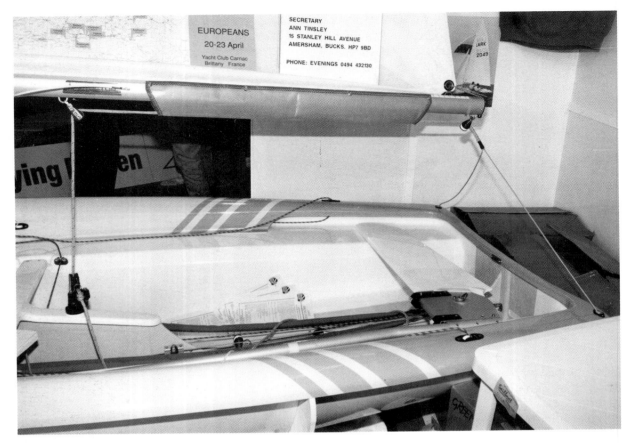

6.11e

Vang

The vang requires a considerable amount of purchase, 16:1 or even 32:1, together with a reasonable amount of throw, since the movement of the boom between a run in light airs and upwind in a breeze is considerable. It also needs to run smoothly with a minimum of friction in both directions, so that when you let it go it eases. If it does not the consequences are at least slow and possibly wet. The four methods of getting the purchase are the cascade, block and tackle, levers and the drum. In fact a combination of two of these is usually the best solution.

As we explained in Chapter 3, mechanical advantage can be obtained with blocks and rope in two ways. The conventional multi-block is both neat and simple. But it does provide a lot of friction for not much purchase, because it needs several blocks. A straight-forward multi-block at 16:1 on a vang would never ease readily enough to work. Whereas the cascade system, doubling the purchase with each extra block, is more efficient, providing more power for less friction. The vang is an ideal place to use it too, as the physical position means the blocks are likely to stay in place and not wrap or twist. The problem with it, is that when the purchase doubles with each block, so does the distance that the whole apparatus needs to move. For instance, if the kicker fixing on the boom moves a foot, the final block in a 32:1 cascade system will need to move 16 feet! Which is longer than most dinghies, and certainly longer than the distance between the base of the mast and the vang take-off point on the boom. If you are going to use a cascade you need to incorporate some clever design.

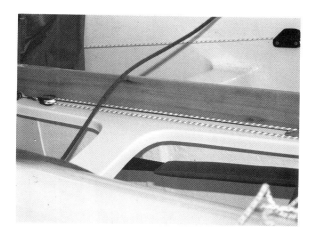

6.12: The final 2:1 purchase of a cascade vang system on a 420 running down the top of the centreboard case. The wire coming from the vang take-off point at the base of the mast can be seen arriving on the top of the centreboard capping on the left of the picture.

One solution is to put two or three parts of the purchase between the boom and the mast, and then the last one or two down the centreboard case (Illustration 6.12). This works well enough, although blocks travelling fore and aft in the bottom of the boat are apt to catch on something. A better solution is to use the cascade combined with either a multi-block or a lever (Illustration 6.13). This is the most popular set-up in a large number of classes. The key to making this work is getting all the lengths correct so you have the full range of adjustment required for upwind in a breeze and downwind in light airs. This used to be difficult when the system had to be made from wire. But, as we will see in Chapter 10, there is no reason why it cannot be done in Spectra, making it much easier to adjust to get the lengths right.

Levers, much like cascades, are highly efficient, releasing easily with a minimum of friction. But again they require a lot of space. Anything much more than a 4:1 purchase lined up in the space between the boom and the centreboard case and most crews will be unable to find a way round it to tack or gybe. In fact the use of levers for the vang is questionable, because of the space they occupy. If you do use one take care that

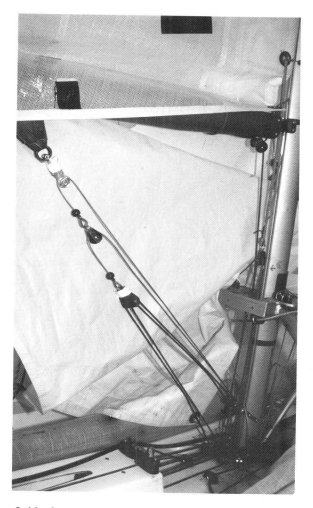

6.13: A combination vang system on an International 14, the 4:1 multi-block on the end of a 4:1 cascade provides 16:1 and fits neatly with enough throw between the mast and the boom.

all the shackles, split rings and so on are well taped over, as it is too easy to hurt yourself on these things. So as with the cascade, with the lever, combine it with a multi-block. A 4:1 lever with a 4:1 multi-block will give you 16:1 and restrict itself to the space between the boom, the mast and boat. Boats that do use these systems effectively, and do not have the problem of space for the crew, are the singlehanders, like the Finn, OK, or Europe dinghies (Illustration 6.14). These use a combination of a lever and a multi-block

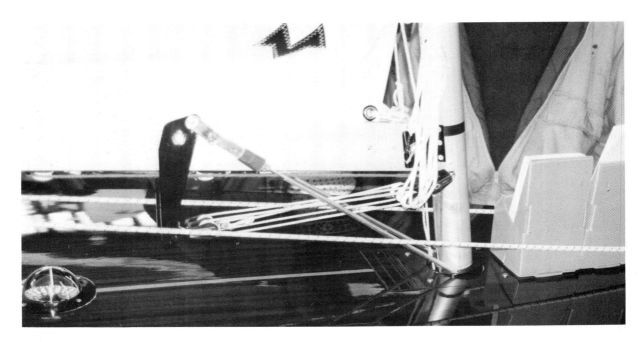

a

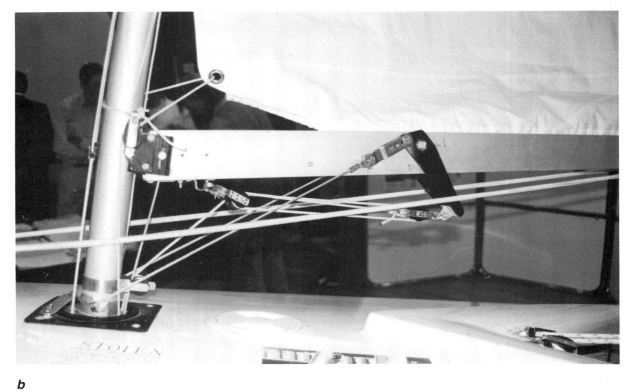

b

6.14: *The vang system on an OK (a) and (b) a Finn. Both use the combination of a neatly mounted lever with a multi-block system.*

system, cleverly engineered to fit into a particularly small space.

The use of drums is quite restricted, mainly because you need a lot of space at the base of the mast which most boats do not have. But if there is room it works efficiently enough, and with the advent of modern cordage, which takes more kindly to wrapping under load than wire does, it should be reliable. In fact the lack of moving parts and splices also helps in the reliability stakes. A point that is important to all these systems, except the drum, is the lead blocks at the base of the mast that direct the tail of the rope aft to the crew or helmsman. When you mount these it is important to take into account the full angle that they will have to work at, ie. both when the boom is in, and fully out to the shroud. If you are not aware of this, the result can make the whole system prone to failure.

Finally, because of the purchase and constant use, the tail of the vang is one of the longest and loosest pieces of rope floating around in the bottom of your boat. Its inclination to wrap around things is second to none (except perhaps for the jib or mainsheets if you do not tie them off). If you are going to put the tail of any rope on an elastic take-up, then the vang is the one to do it with. So this is a good moment to say a few words about them. Elastic take-ups have one purpose, to remove the loose tail of a rope to a quiet area of the boat where it can be held under tension and out of trouble. You can wrap it around a roller that spins to take up the slack, or just tie the tail to a piece of elastic that stretches back down the boat and pulls it tight.

One excellent use of this is to combine it with a continuous system, where the tail of the rope is led to both sides of the boat. From there, the two ends are spliced together. The advantage of this is that if, as happens on a port hand Olympic course, you almost always ease the vang when you bear away on starboard and tension it when you luff up on port, you will never run out of rope. With two individual ends it is easy to round the windward mark in a big gust, go for the vang as you bear away and find you can only ease two inches before you run out of rope. No prizes for guessing what usually happens next. With one loop it is easy enough

6.15: *An elastic take-up on the vang tail, which is also a continuous system. The vang tail is the striped rope coming out of the cam cleat beside the traveller track (on the left of the picture). It runs to the side tank, then down to the floor and back to a pulley. From there it repeats its journey but to the other side of the boat and a separate cleat for the other tack. The turning pulley is on an elastic take-up, which can be seen running away towards the top of the picture. As you pull the vang on through the cam cleats on either side, the elasticated pulley just moves aft to take-up the slack.*

to tie a pulley to it, connect some elastic to this and run it down the boat to take up the slack (Illustration 6.15).

Cunningham

The cunningham is much simpler to organise as it normally needs at most a 4:1 purchase. The exception to this is the fully battened mainsail, when the cunningham will need at least an 8:1. This can usually be arranged between the base of the mast and the cunningham hole on the sail (Illustration 6.16). Like the vang, the cunningham tail can be split and led aft to each side of the boat. It can also have an elastic takeup. But because of the much shorter length of rope involved this can be an unnecessary complication. One neat way of doing it is to lead it to the centreboard capping through a cleat and then a block (Illustration 6.17). The block ensures that which ever angle you pull from it will always jam automatically. Rather than leaving the tail loose, to go down the self bailer, tie it off on something - but check that there is still enough slack to reach it from the hiking position.

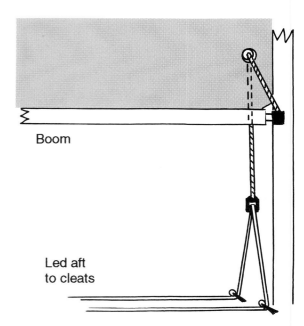

Boom

Led aft
to cleats

6.16: This set-up is almost standard for the cunningham, using a 2:1 with the fixed point at the gooseneck, which is then split again as it is led off to each side, giving you a total of 4:1.

6.17: This is a popular way of leading the cunningham aft to the helmsman. The fairlead ensures that whichever way you pull the rope it will jam in the cleat. Tie the end off so it does not get tangled, but leave enough slack so that you can still reach it from the hiking position.

Outhaul

Ideally there are two functions that the outhaul system should fulfil. The first is fine adjustment for sailing upwind in different wind strengths and sea states. The second is to release a couple of inches quickly when you turn onto a reach. For the first job an 8:1 purchase is about the most you will need. Once the outhaul is attached to the clew it is run back inside the boom. This is probably the neatest place to put the purchase. You can put it after the outhaul exits the boom in the same way that the cunningham is done, but this adds to the clutter in that area of the boat so it is not recommended.

There is plenty of room to run a 4:1 or 8:1 cascade purchase inside the boom, with the tail exiting at the goose neck. From here you can either cleat the line on the boom, or run it aft, to the sidedecks or the centreboard capping perhaps (Illustration 6.18). A refinement of this has one tail of the purchase going to the normal cleat and the other made off on a lever (Illustration 6.19). You then use the clam cleat to make fine adjustments, and the lever to throw off enough outhaul for downwind. At the leeward mark all you have to do is put the lever back on and you have exactly the same outhaul setting as you finished the last beat with. This is probably the most efficient way of meeting the dual requirements for the outhaul.

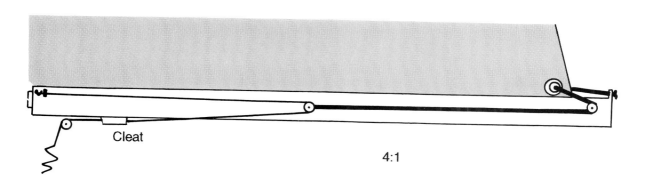

Cleat

4:1

6.18: *A simple outhaul system cleating on the boom. If you use any more than 4:1 it can be difficult to ease the outhaul enough going downwind.*

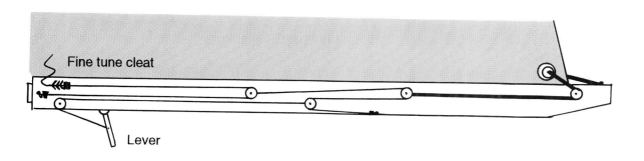

Fine tune cleat

Lever

6.19: *The more sophisticated version, with a lever and fine tune. You can adjust the tension using the 8:1 purchase through the cleat for the beat - with the lever on, and then release the lever downwind.*

There are other methods, if you are happy to have the adjustment on the boom, you can use a Highfield lever (Illustration 3.5) at the exit with a rope coming direct from the sail. The combination of the rack with a lever gives you both fine adjustment and the ability to quickly throw off enough outhaul for the reach. However, it can be tricky to put the outhaul back on quickly, because of the need to line up the lever in the right rack. Also, once you are going upwind fine adjustment means letting the outhaul right off before you can get it back on correctly.

Most of the above applies equally to loose-footed mainsails, except that you will also need an efficient track to slide the clew on. Because of the leech loads a ball bearing track is no bad investment here (Illustration 6.20). The other aspect to all these purchase systems is the attachment to the sail at the clew. The simplest and neatest way to do this is the knot and notch method (Illustration 6.21).

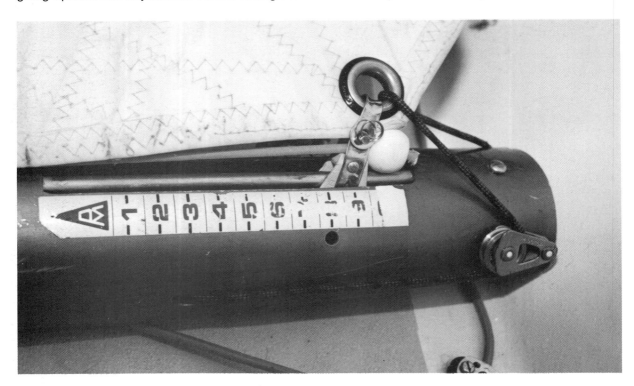

6.20: *The ball bearing outhaul track used on an International 14.*

6.21: *The neatest way to dead-end the outhaul at the clew end, is to cut a notch in the boom, tie a knot in the rope and slip it in. It is particularly easy to undo with cold, wet fingers, but you should keep an eye on the rope near the knot for chafe.*

66

Chapter 7

Foresail Systems

Foresail Sheeting

The foresail on dinghies is usually a jib, although it can be a genoa. The distinction is whether or not the sail comes past the shroud - jibs don't and genoas do. The sail's trim is controlled almost completely by the sheet, both with the tension and the position of the lead. So being able to alter the lead position efficiently is a major factor in good jib trim. Unfortunately the class rules, as in so many other areas, can be restrictive. Two such classes are the Laser II (Illustration 7.1), and the GP14 (Illustration 7.2). No one would willingly choose such restrictive systems - but within the context of a one-design where everyone suffers equally you cannot really complain.

But let us assume that we are sailing a class with broader rules and are allowed to devise something with proper adjustment. The most important initial decision you will make is whether to allow movement fore and aft, laterally or both. Almost certainly you will want to be able to alter the lead fore and aft, usually the question is whether the extra complexity of allowing lateral adjustment is worth the increased trimming ability. There is probably no absolute answer to this one. On yachts where space and weight are less of a consideration the trimming systems use both fore and aft and lateral adjustment. There are certainly times when being able to move the lead outboard or inboard is going to make you quicker. Ultimately it will depend on the particular constraints of the boat, how close you are to the hull weight, whether the internal deck layout allows for a neat solution and so on.

In illustration 7.3 we can see a variety of solutions in different boats. These also include the three basic methods for moving the lead itself. One is to have it on the end of a rope that is pulled up and down, the second is to have it on a car mounted on a track that has pins to stop it in place, and the third is to mount it on a ball bearing car on a track, whose position is

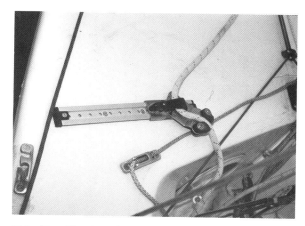

7.1: The jib sheeting system on the Laser II, simple, but impossible to adjust for the tack you are on.

7.2: The jib sheeting system on a GP14, same problem, you can only adjust it with the tension off. Both these classes are limited by the class rules in what they can use.

⇑ **7.3a**   ⇓ **7.3b**

7.3: Solutions to the problem of providing both lateral and fore and aft sheeting adjustment for the jib. On the 505 in (a) the pinned track allows you to move the sheet in and out, although it cannot be adjusted from the windward side. Whilst the sheet lead block is on a rope that is led to windward, allowing you to let it up and down, which has the same effect as moving the lead fore and aft. The Fireball system in (b) uses pinned tracks to provide both lateral and fore and aft adjustment - via height. But you cannot adjust it from the windward side at all. Whilst the Fireball in (c) uses the same lateral adjustment, the height of the lead is controlled by a rope attached to the bottom of the rod and then led to the other side of the boat. The 470 in (d) uses a ball-bearing traveller track for the fore and aft adjustment, with the lead taken from the front of the car to the windward side, and then a short pinned track for lateral adjustment.

⇑ 7.3c

⇓ 7.3d

controlled by rope and elastic. Which of these you choose will come down to all the usual constraints of weight, budget and so on.

The other factor in the decision will be whether you want to adjust the lead from the windward side, or if you are happy to only alter them when they are unloaded. The second scenario makes life a lot simpler, you can use basic tracks with pin stoppers (Illustration 7.4) rather than a whole wallet full of tracks, cleats and blocks. But it is not as efficient when you are sailing. On this one you pay your money and take your choice.

⇑ *7.4a*   ⇓ *7.4b*

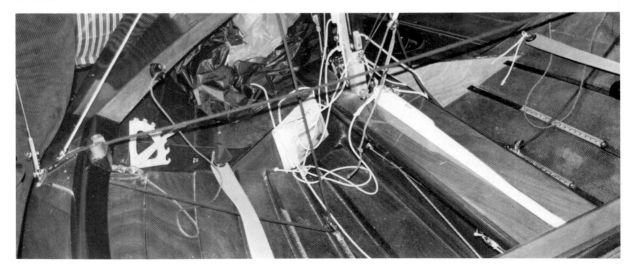

7.4: Simple pinned track adjustment system on (a) an International 14 and (b) a Merlin rocket. The biggest disadvantage is that it cannot be adjusted from the windward side. Notice the way in (b), the jib sheet is led after it has gone through the first block after the sail, this is to make it as easy as possible for the crew to tack the boat - an important consideration.

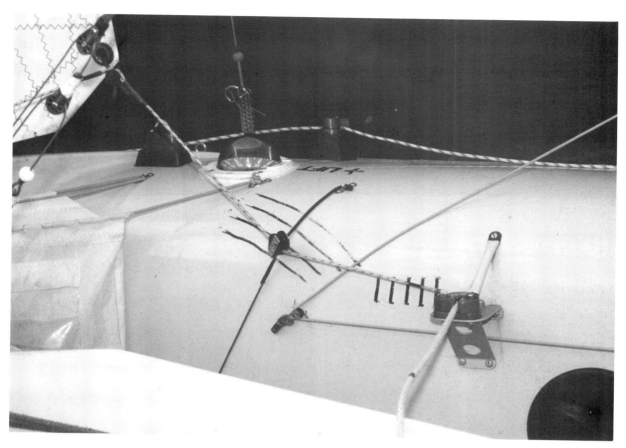

7.5: Jib sheeting system on a 470, the lead block on a rope is led to the other side on a 2:1. It is adjustable fore and aft from to windward, and achieves it with very little equipment. Notice how carefully this is calibrated with a mark for the jib sheet as well.

The system used on many 470's is one of the simplest and lightest (Illustration 7.5). It uses a rope led from the opposite side via a 2:1 purchase. Pull on the rope and it drops the lead, let it go and it raises it. Because of the shape of the 470's tanks it also has the effect of automatically letting the lead go outboard at the same time as it is raised - precisely what you are after. The interesting question about this system is the way that it can move, the block is not solidly fixed to the sidetank and finds the point where the sheet load balances. Going upwind in a breeze the block is inclined to move, but whether this has any detrimental or positive effect on boat speed we do not know. We do know that a lot of people go quickly using it. Care should be taken to pad the tanks, as when the sail flogs it will do its best to

destroy the boat. Ironically, until recently, the 470 class rules forbad this.

If the boat does not have a spinnaker, then you should consider a barber hauler. These enable you to sheet the jib much wider for reaching. The sheet is run through a second block, before the normal upwind lead, that is pulled out to the gunwale using a rope and cleat. Since you can ease the sheet out to do it there is no requirement for a purchase in the system. And you only use them downwind so it is usually unnecessary to run the control line to the opposite side, as you can move to leeward to pull it on without much (if any) loss of speed.

7.6: Jib sheet cleat and turning block mounted on a 505. But using a bullseye fairlead rather than a block will add considerable friction. Another detail to watch in this kind of set up is the gap between the block, or bullseye in this case, and the cleat. It is possible to get the sheet looped round the cleat and jammed between the two fittings if the gap is the wrong size. The result is usually that the sheet jams and you cannot ease the sail. There are three solutions, firstly that the gap is much bigger than the sheet, or much smaller - both of these require moving the fittings. Otherwise you can glue a strip of mylar over the gap between the two, so the sheet cannot drop in.

The other question is what you do with the sheet after it has been through the lead (Illustration 7.4 (b)). This will depend on the boat and the crew's preference for tacking facing forwards or backwards. If you want to face forwards put the final block and cleat near the shrouds, and aft near the traveller if you want to tack facing backwards. The height of the cleat relative to the block is critical for ease of use (Illustration 7.6). On a non-spinnaker boat the sheet should just drop into the cleat when pulled tight across the opposite gunwale. This will give you the best balance between getting it in too easily and not being able to ease it when you are flat-out hiking and hit by a gust. Similarly with a trapeze boat, the sheet should just drop into the cleat when you are at your lowest point on the wire. Although when high wiring in light to moderate breezes this will

make it slightly harder to get in the cleat, it is worth it to be able to flick it out quickly in a breeze.

We have briefly mentioned the idea of using ratchets on the jib sheet. The improvement in the technology of these devices has made them more and more popular. Mostly because you can now switch them off for the lighter breezes. When it is blowing 20 knots and gusty the ability to hold, rather than cleat, the jib and play it properly becomes a big factor in the speed of the boat. And unless you have a high level of fitness you will struggle to maintain that for a two hour championship race without a ratchet.

Foresail Cunningham

These work to exactly the same purpose as the cunningham on the mainsail. They pull the draft of the sail forward and open the leech as the wind increases. At its simplest the jib cunningham consists of a piece of string that ties the sail to the bottom of the jib wire at the tack. The increasing use of stuff luff jibs, where the jib wire pulls out of the sail, has made this popular. The advantages of the stuff luff are that you can keep the same jib wire for different sails - ensuring that you maintain all your rake and tension measurements. It is also a lot easier and less damaging to the modern stiff-clothed sails to roll them without the wire in.

Although these simple cunninghams can be adjusted easily enough on the water, you climb on the foredeck and redo them, it is not possible to adjust it whilst racing. But there is nothing to stop you constructing a more sophisticated version, and leading the control aft (except the class rules of course!). It needs only a 2:1 purchase and a simple cleat back by the mast (Illustration 7.7).

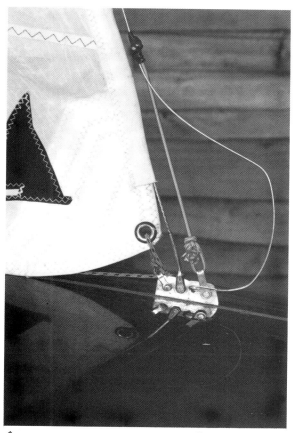

⇑ **7.7a**

7.7: A simple jib cunningham, in (a) you can see it tied off to a separate shackle to the jib wire and forestay, then led through the tack ring in the sail, back down and through a turning block on the deck. It runs aft along the top of the foredeck to the cleat in (b).

⇓ **7.7b**

Foresail Furlers

Where classes allow furlers, which is usually the larger boats with a genoa, it can be a difficult decision whether or not to fit them. In the Flying Dutchman the size of the sail makes it essential, in the International 14 it is marginal (Illustration 7.8). The advantages in seamanship are obvious, getting the sail out of the way makes launching and recovery a lot easier, and also extends the life of the sail. But it raises the height of the tack, and can prevent you from closing the gap between the sail and the foredeck, which is aerodynamically poor. It is also extra weight right in the bow of the boat, along with the accompanying complications of rope and cleats to make it work. It can also fail at critical moments, as Roger Yeoman and Neal McDonald discovered on the FD start line at the 1988 Seoul Olympics. Nevertheless they remain popular in several classes.

⇑ *7.8a*

⇓ *7.8b*

7.8: Jib furling systems, the 505 fitting in (a) does not have a string, which means it can only be furled on the shore, or afloat when sitting on the foredeck. You could launch with it furled though, which would be useful with a fixed rudder. It is a lot smaller and neater than the fitting in (b), on an International 14. Notice here how far up and back the tack of the sail is pushed, compared to its position if the furler were removed.

Chapter 8

Spinnaker Systems

Spinnaker handling systems have perhaps the highest premium on efficiency. If they work well they can save you seconds at mark roundings and that, in a big fleet, can mean many places. Getting the gear set-up for quick hoists, gybes and drops can be a regatta winner. The first step is the division of labour during the various manoeuvres. Who is going to pull the halyard up and put the pole out in a hoist? Who controls the sheets through a gybe? You must think through the manoeuvres carefully, placing all the cleats and pulleys where they will come most easily to the right person's hands. And remember, the real enemy of the system is friction, and it should be eliminated wherever possible.

Halyard

Your first decision is to decide who is going to pull the halyard up, and clear it to run free when the spinnaker comes back down. Nine times out of ten, or even ninety nine out of a hundred it will be the helmsman. Generally the division of labour in a hoist and drop is that the helmsman pulls the spinnaker up and down whilst the crew does the pole.

There are two occasions when it might be different. The first is with an asymmetric or symmetric spinnaker where the pole is fully automatic and launched by a rope, so it can be led back to the helmsman just as easily. Since it is then the quickest job it makes sense to give it to the helmsman, and move the halyard forward to the crew. The second circumstance is with spinnaker bags, where the halyard cleat can be placed on the floor near the mast with a foot operated trip system. This enables the crew to let the halyard go when he wants to pull the spinnaker down, rather than relying on an often distracted helmsman to watch what he is doing and release it for him.

Both these cases are a minority, and for most boats the consideration is how the helmsman

a

b

c

8.1: *Spinnaker halyard cleats, in (a) with a simple bullseye and clam cleat. In (b) on the back end of the centreboard case capping on a 505. The spinnaker halyard, a white rope with dark flecking, is led from the floor and up through the upside down cam cleat. The version in (c) has put the block behind the cleat, which ensures that the halyard jams wherever it is pulled from.*

can pull twenty-odd feet of rope through a pulley as fast as possible. The second consideration is getting the twenty-odd feet of rope back through the pulley at least as quickly without it tying in a knot. There are three lines of thinking on this one. The first is that you just pull like hell, hand over hand with the tiller between your knees. In this case the halyard set-up is straight-forward, several versions are shown in illustration 8.1. It is best to have the halyard marked so that you know the sail is at the top of the mast without having to look up at the masthead.

The disadvantage is that if you cannot get both hands into action, it will be a pretty slow hoist, as there will be three or four handfuls each of which mean changing your grip. And even if you do get both hands on it you will have poor control of the boat while you hoist, which in a stronger breeze or a big fleet can be dangerous. The third disadvantage is that if you do not have a chute where the halyard becomes the retrieval line there is a length of rope lying loose in the boat which will almost invariably get tangled. This will have an inevitable result when you come to dropping the spinnaker.

We will come onto retrieval systems next, but briefly if you use a spinnaker chute you will have a line attached to the middle of the spinnaker to pull it into the chute. This line is then run continuously through the boat to become the spinnaker halyard. So that as you pull the spinnaker up, the halyard disappears back out of the boat attached to the middle of the spinnaker - keeping the amount of loose rope in the boat to a minimum.

If you use spinnaker bags there will be no retrieval line and using the simple halyard hoist leaves you with all that rope in the boat. One solution is to use a halyard take-up. This is an elastic driven device that takes-up the slack in the halyard as fast as you can create it. There are several variations on this theme, at its simplest you splice a piece of elastic onto the tail of the halyard and run it up and down the boat through blocks. A more sophisticated version was mentioned in Chapter 3. This uses a drum that is powered by elastic to wind up the spare halyard. These are all reasonable solutions to the problem of the loose rope, but they still do not address the fact that you need two hands for a quick hoist.

One answer is to go for a pump halyard system. This uses a special cleat combined with a strong elastic take-up to enable you to hoist one-handed (Illustration 8.2). The pump system does work well, but it needs to be set up carefully. The elastic tension, angle of the cleats and blocks are all critical. If you get it right it works marvellously. If you get it wrong it can be worse than useless, with the elastic not taking up the slack you have to resort to a straight pull. The loops of rope that gather are almost guaranteed to knot. But when it is working it does answer the requirements completely. You can pull up the spinnaker with one hand, and the halyard tail is kept neatly ready for the spinnaker to come down. On the drops you have to pull it down a little harder than otherwise, because you are working against the elastic take-up, but at least it should not foul.

8.2a

8.2b

8.2c

8.2d

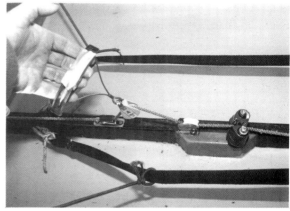

8.2e

8.2: *The pump spinnaker halyard system runs back through the boat from the base of the mast, through a cleat and pulley and on through a handle followed by the pump cleat (a). It then runs to the side of the cockpit and is woven through a multi-block system attached to a long, strong piece of elastic (b), before being tied off on a becket on the multi-block. The pump cleat works like a valve, not allowing the halyard that has already passed through it as the spinnaker is pulled up, to go back the other way. So as you pull upwards on the handle (c), the spinnaker is pulled up because the pump cleat will not allow the spare halyard to be pulled back through it. You then ease on the handle, and the elastic driven block system takes up the slack in the halyard that you have just pulled through from the mast (d). The normal jamming cleat not allowing the spinnaker to pull it back down and the pump cleat this time allowing the elastic block system to pull the halyard into the back of the boat. The effect is that you pull the halyard up with one hand on the handle, the pump system taking up the slack for you each time, ready for another pull. The clever part is that whilst the pump cleat will not allow the halyard to go back out through it on the hoist, you can still get the spinnaker down. This is the reason you need the special pump cleat seen in (e) with 'Northfix' written on it. It will let the rope pass either way when it is flat, only jamming the halyard from going out when it is pulled up at an angle by the pump handle pulling the halyard up. So to let the spinnaker down you just flick it out of the forward cleat and down it comes.*

The other solution that fulfils all this, but does it more simply, is the reverse purchase. It follows from our mechanical principles in Chapter 3, that if we run a purchase the other way around we will increase the load on a rope, but also decrease the amount of rope that has to be pulled. And this is the technique for the spinnaker halyard, where the load, at least when the spinnaker is not filling, is minimal. The problem instead is that there is too much of it to pull in one handful. You can half the amount by putting a 1:2 purchase on the halyard (Illustration 8.3). On most boats this will reduce the spinnaker hoist to one big pull, you can put another purchase in to shorten it even more if this is not enough. But any more than 1:3 and the loads become a serious problem if the spinnaker ever gets stuck.

The big advantage of the system is simplicity. There is little to go wrong. Although it does leave a loose tail in the bottom of the boat it is short enough not to be capable of much damage. On the drops it is possible to pull the whole tail through the final pulley before you uncleat it, so it is guaranteed to run clear. The one thing you should watch out for is the pulley running up and down the boat, it is more likely to get caught than the halyard alone. Try and arrange a clear path for it when you place the lead blocks at either end of the boat.

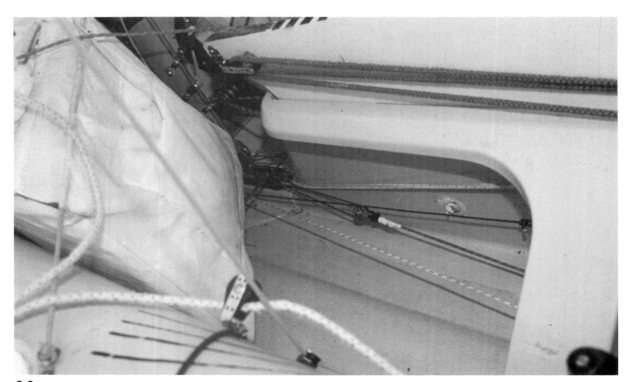

8.3a

8.3: The 1:2 spinnaker halyard system, where the halyard runs out of an exit at the base of the mast, through a block and then ties off at the mast foot (a - the pulley is beside the centreboard case with white tape around the top). Attached to this block is a line which runs to the back of the boat, through a block and then forward to the back of the centreboard case area, where it goes through a cleat and then a pulley that acts as a lead (b). The block travels to the back of the boat (as it has between pictures (a) and (b)) taking the halyard with it - so for every foot that you pull on this line, the spinnaker halyard will go up two feet. This is shown diagrammatically in (c).

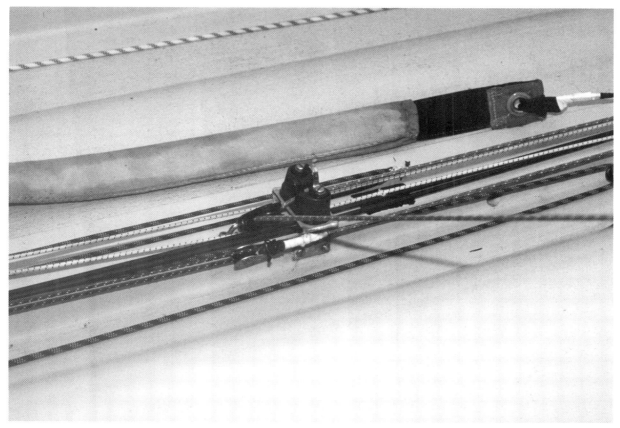

8.3b

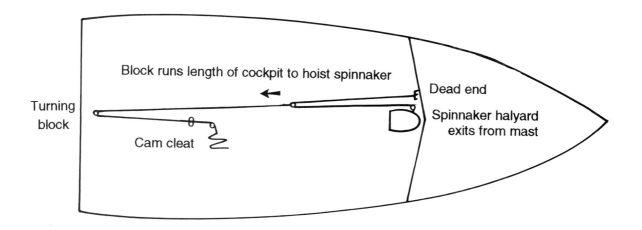

Block runs length of cockpit to hoist spinnaker

Dead end

Turning block

Spinnaker halyard exits from mast

Cam cleat

8.3c

Retrieval

So much for pulling the spinnaker up, how are you going to get it down again? There are two choices, you can either pull the spinnaker into a chute with the opening at the bow, using a retrieval line (Illustration 8.4), or you can pull it down hand over hand and put it in some kind of bag (Illustration 8.5). As we have already noted, the choice you make here is going to have an impact on the halyard system. If you choose a chute it provides a ready made take-up system for the halyard slack. But given the effective solutions that we have outlined for this problem it should not be a factor in your chute/bag decision.

The considerations are two-fold, boat handling and speed. In the hands of equally competent crew, there is no doubt that the chute should provide faster spinnaker drops and about even hoists. But there is a boat speed penalty to pay. The engineering required for the chute will add weight to the front of the boat. Having an opening at the bow will also allow water into the boat every time you stick the bow in a wave, soaking the spinnaker and filling up the boat. It also punishes the spinnaker a lot more, hauling it in and out of the chute, which wears it out faster. The choice you make may well depend on the quality of your crew. If they are good enough to almost remove the differences in handling between the chute and the bags, the bags will be quicker round the race track. If they are not particularly good or familiar with using bags, then the chute will be a safer and probably faster choice.

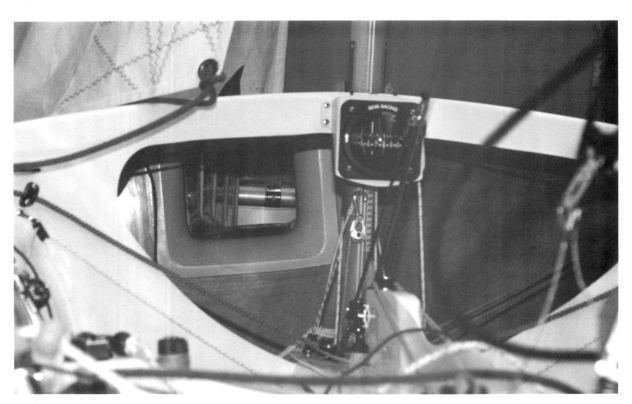

8.4: Looking up the spinnaker chute on a 505.

8.5: Spinnaker bags on a 420, the spinnaker is always pulled into the windward bag.

If you decide on the bags there is little to add to the boat beyond the bags themselves. Usually there is one on each side of the boat with the spinnaker being pulled down into the windward one. They should be enclosed, complete bags which will stop the spinnaker falling out and getting pulled into other control lines. They should also have net bottoms so they will drain, and elasticated tops to hold the sail into the bag. One important tweak is the system to hold the halyard in place. Ideally this should stop the halyard coming out and wrapping itself round the shroud when you are sailing along, but allow it to be pulled out when you want to hoist the spinnaker. There are a couple of solutions to this one, the simplest is the plastic clip (Illustration 8.6). But sometimes these are not strong enough, particularly if you have a pump system where the elastic is

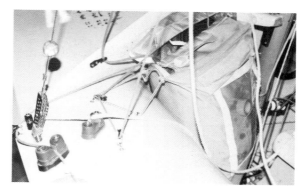

8.6: The spinnaker halyard is tucked into a black plastic clip on the washboard at the top of the picture. The way this one is mounted it would be impossible to hoist the spinnaker without unclipping the halyard first. But if they are mounted with the open end upwards you can hoist the halyard by just pulling.

8.7: If the plastic clip in 8.6 does not prove strong enough, then this is an alternative, the elasticated bar holds the halyard in place.

always trying to hoist the spinnaker for you. The second solution is a bar attached to the shroud plate and held down by elastic - this version can be beefed up as much as necessary to keep the halyard in place (Illustration 8.7).

A chute requires a little more complexity, not only do you need the chute itself, but also the retrieval line to pull the spinnaker into it. For most of us, with one-design, production or second-hand boats, the chute design is not something we can change. If you do have an option, the wider the mouth and the fairer the surface the better. Most chutes have a wood or plastic mouth and some have a cloth sock attached, rather than just leaving the spinnaker loose under the foredeck. The advantages of the sock are that it keeps the spinnaker under control when it is in the boat, and stops it falling into control systems - particularly when you are capsized. The disadvantage is just the weight of the sock and the water it holds in the spinnaker. For this reason if you do fit a sock the material is important. It should allow the spinnaker to drain, and not absorb much water itself. But at the same time it should not be stretchy. Otherwise it will allow the spinnaker, particularly if it is new, stiff cloth and the chute is smaller than it should be, to expand in a bunch behind the back of the plastic chute - making it almost impossible to hoist. Making the top of the sock from a material such as mylar will both prevent

this and, as it is slippery it will help the spinnaker out of the chute. Another tweak is to ensure that the inboard end of the chute sock is closed with a ringlet that only the rope can exit through. If you pull the spinnaker, and particularly the retrieval patch, out through the narrow end of the sock it will take you an extra minute to get it back through next time you hoist. Obviously the sock should be long enough that when you hit this ringlet the sail is right inside the boat.

The retrieval line is relatively straight-forward, just attaching to the centre of the spinnaker and running down into the chute and out the other end, where it goes into the spinnaker halyard system as discussed above. Two points to be made. The first is the position and number of the patches that attach the retrieval line to the spinnaker. With small spinnakers one patch is normally sufficient, it should be in the centre and the line should be attached to the outside to help keep the spinnaker out of the water as it comes down. Twin patches, at one and two thirds height will help with bigger, perhaps asymmetric spinnakers. It has two effects, one is to keep the bottom section of the spinnaker in the chute and out of the water. The other is to spread the spinnaker out along the chute by pulling in two places, which helps to stop it bunching.

The second point is that you will need an extra pulley at the back of the chute to give you a good lead when pulling the spinnaker down. With the big asymmetric spinnakers on the International 14's the retrieval line is often lead to a block on the dagger-board case so the crew can get their whole body and two arms swinging on it. With smaller spinnakers you may not need quite such a concentrated effort, but you should at least be able to access it easily from both sides of the boat.

Another modification that works well on 505's and may be adaptable to other boats is to elasticate the end of the chute or the sail back under the foredeck (Illustration 8.8) to get it out of the way. You can pull the sail into the chute easily enough, but as soon as you release the retrieval line the elastic, attached to the forward bulkhead, takes the sail up under the foredeck leaving the cockpit clear.

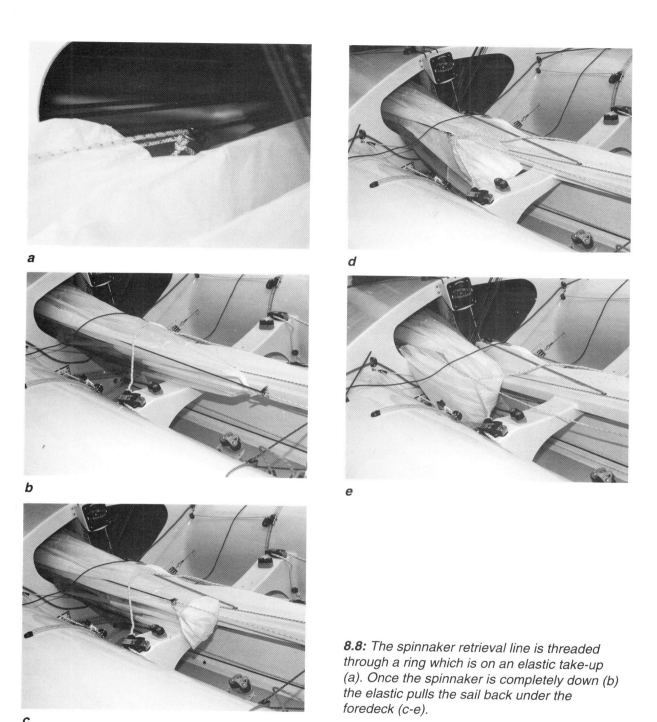

8.8: *The spinnaker retrieval line is threaded through a ring which is on an elastic take-up (a). Once the spinnaker is completely down (b) the elastic pulls the sail back under the foredeck (c-e).*

Sheets and Guys

At its simplest the spinnaker sheeting arrangement for a dinghy is that used for asymmetrics. The lead runs from the sail to a block at the back of the boat. For good sail trim this should be as far aft and outboard as the boat and the rules will allow. The disadvantage of this is that if the boom is short you will stand a good chance of catching the sheet over the top of it in a gybe. This is inevitably slow and often wet as well. You can tie a safety elastic from the leech of the main to the end of the boom to help prevent this happening, but you may also need to move the leads a little way forward.

From there the sheet goes forward to a turning block about opposite where the crew will sit or trapeze when sailing downwind. Unless it is a ridiculously small sail, or you have a particularly large crew, this should always be a ratchet block. You can switch the ratchet off when you do not need it after all. From there it goes to a similar block on the opposite tank and then off to the back of the boat and the clew of the sail. This works fine when all you need is two sheets, something more is required to turn the windward sheet into a guy when you have a symmetrical spinnaker.

The simplest way to do this is to have a hook and cleat up by the shroud (Illustration 8.9). This allows you to pin the guy under the hook and then cleat it off. At its simplest this hook is just an extended shroud pin with a smooth bearing surface. The cleat behind it can be a cam or clam cleat. The two things you should be wary of, are that the cleat is high enough relative to the hook so that the guy is not just pulled through or out when it loads up. And secondly that the sheet does not drop in the cleat accidentally. This can be corrected by glueing mylar strips in place, that drop over the jaws and hold the sheet out unless you want it in.

The next step up in complexity is the twinning lines, or twing lines as they are sometimes known. This replaces the hook with a block on the spinnaker sheet and a line run to a separate cleat. It works like a barber hauler - when you pull it on and jam it the sheet is held to the deck - free to run, but pinned to the deck just like it was under the hook (Illustration 8.10). At its

a

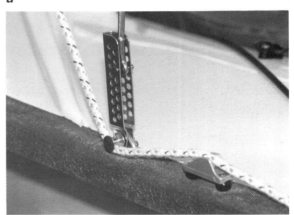

b

8.9: *A simple hook (a) under which to place the spinnaker sheet in order to turn it into the spinnaker guy. And in (b) the hook for the spinnaker guy is the extension of the pin on the shroud adjuster.*

simplest the twinning line is one continuous line between the two sheets, as you uncleat the old windward side going into the gybe, you pull the new windward one on. As with the hook and cleat the crucial thing is getting the twinning line block low enough for the jammer to work properly - this can mean both raising the cleat and a lot of searching in chandleries for the right block. You will also need to have mylar covers on both the twinning line and guy cleats to stop them going in accidentally. Try pulling the leeward twinner on a couple of feet on a reach, sometime when the result does not matter, and you will see why.

a

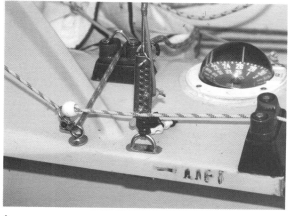

b

8.10: *A twinning (or twinging) line on an FD. In (a), it is pulled on and the spinnaker guy is held down tight to the deck. It can now be jammed in the cam cleat positioned just aft of it. Notice the mylar strips used to cover the cleat and stop the guy dropping in accidentally. Seen on a 470 in (b), the cam cleat to the left of the shroud is jamming the twinning line on, holding the guy down, which is in turn cleated in the cam cleat to the right of the shroud. Notice how the cleats are all mounted on blocks to ensure that the load from the rope is down and into the cleat.*

One simple but effective modification of this is to add a stopper to both sides of the sheet that comes up against the twinning line block when the guy is eased as far forward as the pole on the forestay. This means you can go through a reach to reach gybe and all you have to do with the new guy is make sure the twinning line is on. That presets it to the right point to get the sail full and the boat moving away from the mark (Illustration 8.11).

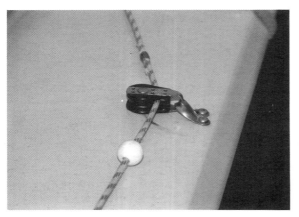

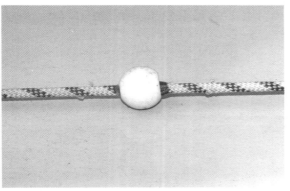

8.11: *Stoppers on the spinnaker sheets, the bobble is threaded on the sheet between the aft block and the twinning line block. The sheet is then overstitched so that it will run through the aft block (a) but not the bobble (b). The bobble in turn cannot go through either block, so when stitching meets bobble meets twinning line block (c) the guy cannot go forward any further. The stitching needs to be carefully positioned so that this leaves the pole just off the forestay.*

A further modification is to lead the twinning lines aft to the helmsman so that he controls them through a gybe. The crew is usually pre-occupied with getting the pole across in this manoeuvre and the division of labour can be beneficial. The system is no more complex, it just means running two separate twinning lines aft. But if you leave them forward there is a rather more complex tweak that allows the crew to do both twinning lines through a starboard to port gybe just by pulling one rope. It is only worth doing if you race a lot on port hand triangles, but it can make gybing incredibly quick. All it requires is a further fairlead set inboard of the twinning line cleat on the port side. The lead should be such that when you pull the twinning line through this fairlead it drops it into the cleat. On the starboard side you have a rope handle attached to a block that is running on the twinning line itself - inboard of the twinning line cleat. It should be elasticated in place close to the windward tank. Coming

into the gybe you grab the rope handle and pull upwards, the windward twinner is pulled out of the cleat and the leeward one into its cleat by the one action - presto one gybe completed. Another more common modification is the addition of a cleat by the mid-boat turning blocks for use on the guy (Illustration 8.12). These are popular on some non-trapeze dinghies where the crew sits on the guy rather than putting it under a shroud hook. The inboard cleat then becomes the only one used on the guy. But if you have a shroud hook and cleat or twinners these jammers are extraneous, we have only ever used them when the shroud cleat has broken. When they are used the risk of flicking them out accidentally is quite high. They add weight in the middle of the boat, which can be a plus if you need it, but if you do not and they are not part of your regular sail handling techniques, you might as well leave them off.

a

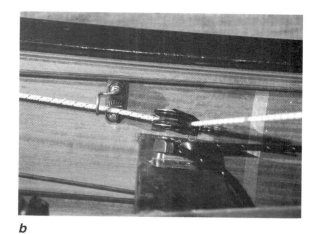

b

8.12: *Inboard guy cleats arranged so that the cleat only works when the sheet is pulled vertically - as a guy from the same side (a), rather than as a sheet from the opposite side (b).*

Symmetric Pole Systems

Pole systems can be graded in terms of complexity, at the bottom is the detached pole that the rules insist you use on a 470. Next up are the boom-stowed double-ended poles that are launched by hand, followed by boom-stowed single-ended poles, either single or pairs, with or without elastic take-aways and automatic launchers. As we will see there are several variations on each of these themes. Finally there is the full twin pole system with sheets attached, but this is so complex and rarely used we could not find any boats to take pictures of!

Starting at the bottom we have the detachable pole seen on the 470 (Illustration 8.13). This uses a piston at both ends to attach it to the guy and the mast (Illustration 8.14), along with a hook in the middle to attach it to the uphaul/downhaul. When not being used the pole stores in the bottom of the boat. The other area for consideration, which applies to all of the other systems, is the uphaul/downhaul control.

The uphaul/downhaul system has two requirements, that it be elasticated to bring it up tight against the mast when not in use, and that its upwards movement when it is in use be limited to stop the pole skying on a reach. The simplest way to achieve this is to have the uphaul run from the pole to the sheave on the mast, then down to the mast foot and off to a cleat,

8.13: *A 470 spinnaker pole, which is completely detachable from the rest of the system, hanging on the uphaul/downhaul hook. The centre hook is a trade-off between being able to get it on and off quickly on the hoists and drops and not having it fall off when you are gybing. At the first extreme you have an open hook, at the other it closes completely with a spring. The one shown is a compromise. One particularly good point about this type of hook is that it ties at the top and bottom, rather than just in the middle. This prevents it from pivoting, since if it can move upwards in a gust you will lose power. The connection point to the mast can be seen just above the pole. The pole clips onto both this and the guy with a piston end fitting (8.14).*

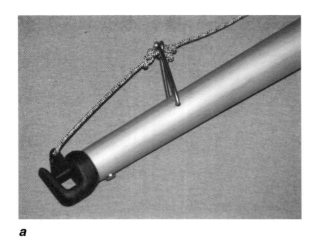

a

d

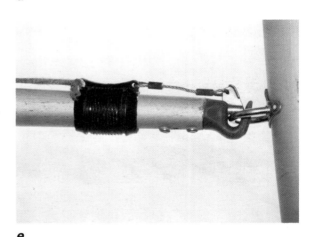

b

e

c

8.14: *Various options for the piston ends; it is a matter of personal choice here, as to which you can use quickest. Personally we like the triggers (a) and (b), since they only require that you grab the pole with one hand, rather than holding it still with one and pulling the string with the other; (c) and (d) show the 'Fico' pole end and (e) is a variation on the trigger theme.*

from which the pole height can be adjusted. Whether this cleat is on the mast, led to the centreboard capping or divided and taken to both sides of the boat is individual choice - with all the normal trade-offs of weight and efficiency against simplicity and reliability. The downhaul runs to the base of the mast, through a block and onto the elastic take-up. To stop the pole skying you tie a stopper knot in front of the block at the pole's maximum height position.

The problem with this system is that it is not completely positive except when the pole is at its maximum height. The spinnaker is only working against the downhaul elastic take-up most of the time, and any decent gust will see the pole sky upwards a little, which is throwing away the power you need to drive forwards.

The solution to this is to have a positive downhaul with a take-up, ie. a rope that runs from the pole via the mast foot to a cleat, but with an elasticated pulley between the two. The elastic takes the slack out of the rope in front of the cleat when the pole is not being used (Illustration 8.15). This locks the pole in place completely - the only disadvantage is that to adjust the height you have to let one cleat go and pull another on. A solution to that is to have the uphaul and downhaul as one continuous rope which is adjusted between reversed cleats. So you can pull it either way with one hand, and as you let it go it will just drop back into both cleats. How and where you arrange all this will depend on the internal layout of the boat.

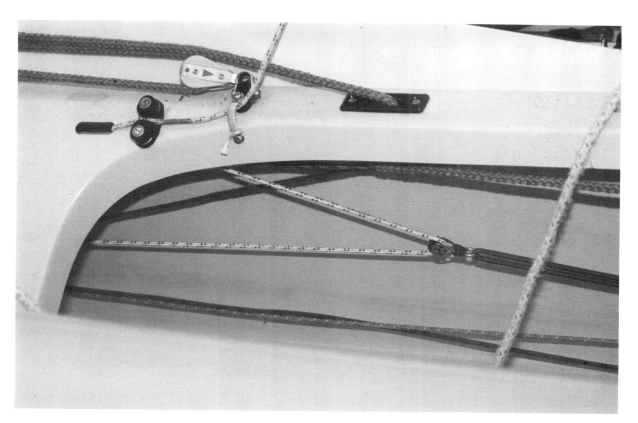

8.15: *Elasticated take-up on the spinnaker pole downhaul. The pole is not in position here and the pulley and elastic is pulling the downhaul aft and taking all the slack out. When the pole is clipped on the downhaul comes tight and leads straight from the mast foot through the hole in the centreboard capping to the cleat. The pad-eye behind the cleat is to ensure that it jams wherever you pull the downhaul from. The string round it is to protect the crew from ripping sailing gear on it.*

The next step up in pole technology is to stow it alongside the boom. The critical aspect of this is the positions of the pole eye and the uphaul sheave on the mast (Illustration 8.16). It is a function of the geometry of pole and boom, but the objective is that when the pole is at its normal launched height it should lie horizontally alongside the boom when stowed. You still use piston ends at both ends of the pole, the only difference to the detachable pole is the uphaul/downhaul arrangement. This was done with the keyhole, where a block on the pole fits through a metal ring, but when half-twisted is not allowed back - locking it in place in the launched position, but this has generally been superseded by a rope loop in the uphaul/downhaul and a plastic ramp on the pole (Illustration 8.17) which is much more effective.

8.16a

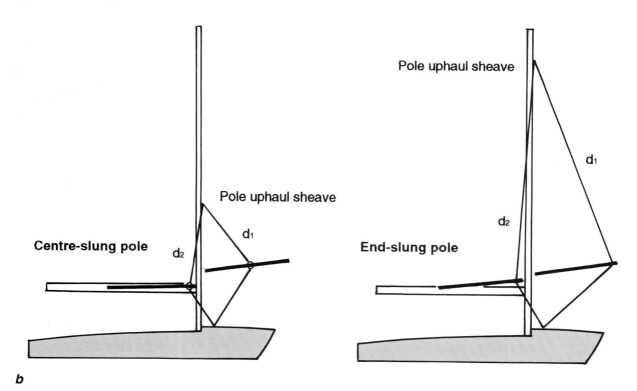

b

8.16: *Spinnaker pole stowed along the boom in (a), and in (b) we can see that to get the pole to lie neatly parallel to the boom, distance d1 needs to equal distance d2. The position of the pole eye and the uphaul sheave will probably be controlled by the class rules, so you must juggle them within these constraints to try to achieve this. Notice the difference in pole uphaul sheave height between an end slung pole and a centre slung pole. Do not forget to take into account the angle you normally fly the pole at.*

8.17: The ramp system on the spinnaker pole allows the pole to be pushed out till the loop in the uphaul/downhaul catches in the notch, locking the pole in place. To stow the pole it is half-turned to disengage the rope loop from the notch then pulled back into place along the boom.

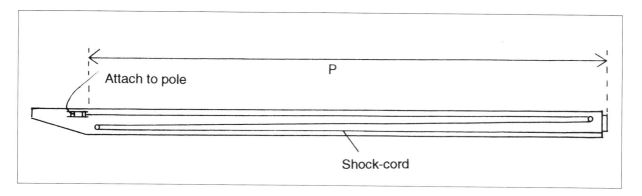

8.18: The sheave in the boom for the retrieval elastic must be mounted at least as far back as the length of the pole 'P'. The elastic must then be run up and down the boom twice to give enough stretch. Note that the sheave should be mounted as high as possible in the boom to help keep the pole out of the helm's way when it is stowed. It is sometimes worth putting a bullseye lead in front of the sheave, to prevent the elastic fraying on the edge of the sheave when the pole is stowed.

The next step up is to fix an elastic retractor, so that although the pole is still launched by hand, when unclipped from the mast it is pulled back in along the boom by the elastic. This is usually done with an elastic take-up hidden inside the boom (Illustration 8.18). Although the pole has double piston ends and is manually launched, it can only be used as a single-end pole through a gybe because of the retractor elastic. So you have to gybe by taking the pole off the mast and guy, then retrieve it from behind the mainsail after the gybe.

There are several consequences of this, firstly you need to have the uphaul and downhaul fixed in place at the end of the pole. This allows you to fire away the pole and let it stow without disconnecting the ramp system described above. Once the pole is stowed the uphaul/downhaul will hold the outboard end neatly in place by the boom. It also means the pole can be lighter as it is only subjected to compressive loadings. But because of the problem with relaunching the pole after a gybe you need one of two further modifications to make it worth having the retractor elastic. Firstly you can fit a string launcher, which saves you having to fumble around on the leeward side of the boom after the gybe, by giving you a line to pull that will relaunch the pole. Secondly you

can have two poles, each with their own elastic retractors and downhauls.

The second of these, the twin pole system, is the easiest to describe - simply duplicate the system we have already talked about. The first option, the string launcher, is a little more complex, and the key to it is the fitting on the mast. Rigging the string to launch the pole is simple enough, it attaches at the inboard end of the pole and runs to the mast where the inboard end attaches. Here you can have just a block, which then takes the line down the mast and into the boat - to wherever you want to site the launch line. Either the crew or the helm can have the control, but obviously it must be accessible from both sides of the boat. The problem with the block is that it does not provide a particularly solid fixing for the base of the pole, and it is important that the launch line gets pulled tight to keep it in place. A better, but more expensive solution, is the Spiro fitting (Illustration 8.19) which is specially developed for the job. It combines both a roller for the string and a solid mast to pole fixing. A useful detail with this is to mount it slightly offset to port on the mast. This helps it to flick free and retract when you are dropping on the port gybe and the pole wants to go the wrong side of the mast.

a

b

8.19: The Spiro fitting which allows the string launcher to pull the pole out on the roller (a), where the bobble drops into place and holds it firm (b).

The other possibility is both simple and effective to use, particularly when combined with forks at the outboard end of the pole, as is found on many 505s. This uses a manual launch and inboard piston end but the elastic only directs which side of the boom the pole goes, rather than pulling it into place (Illustration 8.20). Going through the gybe involves only flicking the inboard end off the mast, and directing it down the leeward side of the boom. The guy just drops out of the fork. On the new gybe you put the new guy back in the fork and relaunch the pole clipping it on the mast.

8.20a

8.20: *Spinnaker pole system seen on a 505. The uphaul and downhaul are permanently fixed in place and the pole lies slung on a piece of elastic that runs from the end of the boom, round the front of the mast slightly above the pole eye and back to the end of the boom (a). The pole is attached via a ring in (b). In (c) we can see the pole launched and clipped to the mast with a conventional piston end. Although the system on this boat does not have it, you can use a fork for the guy (d). This speeds up gybing at the risk of it disengaging when you do not want it to, the risk depends on the geometry of the rest of the spinnaker system. It works well on 505's but has not caught on in other classes.*

8.20b

8.20c

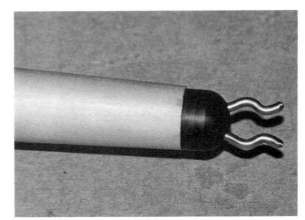

8.20d

Asymmetric Pole Systems

At the moment only a few classes use asymmetric spinnakers, and most of these systems have been developed from the International 14. If we ignore the Australian skiffs, the I14 has led the recent trend towards setting big masthead gennakers tacked down on a pole extending beyond the bow of the boat. The distinction with the skiffs is that they use a fixed pole, which for practical purposes most classes in the Northern hemisphere (I14, Cherub and 405) have substituted with a retractable system.

The size and shape of these sails necessitates that the handling systems work efficiently. One reason for this not being the case is block failure, which is sometimes difficult to detect when the equipment is not under load. Experience with the I14's has shown this to be a depressingly regular occurrence because of the extremely high loads - especially when retrieving a water-logged spinnaker. It is worth using the highest specification blocks you can afford, or find, in the key areas of the system. And of course doing regular maintenance checks.

Depending on the length of the pole and its construction, it is sometimes necessary to fit a bobstay as the upward lift forces generated by these sails are significant. This can usually be incorporated into the tack downhaul system for the spinnaker, as shown in illustration 8.21. This system is favoured on boats using parallel poles, although tapered poles have been developed which are light, stiff and strong enough to be used without the support of the bobstay.

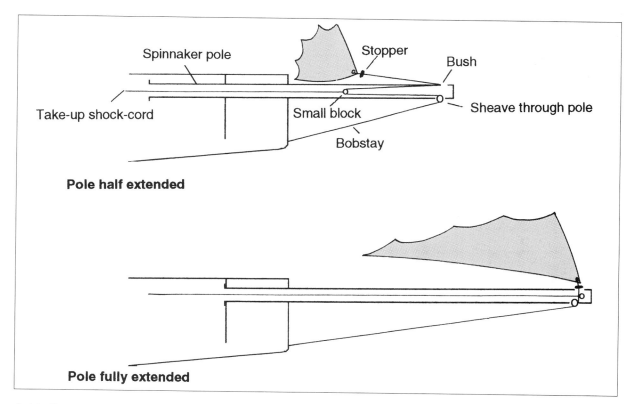

Pole half extended

Pole fully extended

8.21: The bobstay is continuous with the spinnaker tack downhaul and is held taut when the pole is fully extended and the stopper knot reaches the bush in the top of the pole. Note the use of a bush rather than a sheave here, because when the spinnaker is set from port to starboard the direction of pull will vary and a sheave will wear through the wire or rope.

a

b

8.22: *In (a) we can see an asymmetric pole front bearing, on an I14, note the Teflon tape lining. The asymmetric pole aft bulkhead bearing on an I14 in (b) is made from nylon to reduce friction.*

If the pole is retractable it effectively runs through a hole in the hull by the bow and a bulkhead just aft of the bow. Needless to say these have to be well engineered to take the loads. The surfaces of the bearing apertures are best lined with sticky-back nylon or Teflon tape as the less friction here the quicker and easier it is to pull out the pole (Illustration 8.22). The advantages of the tapered pole are that you do not have to worry about it binding if it is not perfectly straight. This can be a big problem with parallel poles even if they are only slightly bent.

As with all spinnaker work the speed of the hoist and drop is vital, so the pole launching and halyard system must be carefully planned out. Since these spinnakers are almost always used with a chute there is no need for a halyard take-up, as it forms the retrieval line. The division of labour is important and it often pays to have a system which enables the helm and crew to do either task in the hoist. Unless circumstances are unusual the crew always does both jobs on the takedown. The solution most commonly seen on the I14 is to lead both the pole launching system and the halyard down the top of the board casing. Both systems automatically cleat at the front of the casing (Illustration 8.23) when pulled through blocks leading to either crew or helmsman. This means that if control is getting marginal and the helmsman wants to concentrate on keeping the boat upright or not hitting things, the crew can do both the pole and the spinnaker.

8.23: *The top of the dagger board case on an I14, with the pole outhaul cleat on the left at the front of the casing and the spinnaker halyard on the right. Note the pole sock running down the left side and the spinnaker chute running down the right.*

Alternatively in a less stressful hoist the tasks can be split. Some people favour the pole being pulled out by the helm. There is not much rope to pull so it takes less time and is less distraction from steering. If the helm stops hoisting the spinnaker half-way because he needs a hand on the tiller the spinnaker is almost bound to end up in the water. If he stops launching the pole half-way the consequences are much less dramatic. It is the safest technique but not the fastest. This is because when the spinnaker is hoisted by the crew, once it is up he still has to pick up the sheet, pull it in, clip on to the trapeze and get out. A few more seconds before you can luff up and get the power on and get moving. If the crew launches the pole and the helm hoists the spinnaker the crew will be finished first (or certainly should be!) and can already have the sheet in his hand and be clipped on ready to go the second the kite is fully hoisted.

When dropping the spinnaker it is almost always best for the crew to do the whole job. It is a set of physically demanding and critically timed tasks with a particular order. It would be extremely difficult for the helmsman to do whilst steering. You must first take out the slack in the spinnaker downhaul, then uncleat the halyard, pull it into the chute as far as it will go, then uncleat the pole and finish pulling on the downhaul. If you get the order or timing wrong you will end up with the spinnaker in the water - then it is an early swim or a trip to the bow as though it was a 40 foot keel boat.

The most popular pole system is shown in illustration 8.24 where a 1:1 system is used on the pole outhaul. This also pulls out the spinnaker tack downhaul and provides a shock cord return on the pole. A variation is to have the spinnaker tack permanently attached to the end of the pole so that when the spinnaker is pulled back into the chute this also pulls back the pole. The disadvantage is that the spinnaker is left sticking out over the bow where it can scoop up water as you are sailing along upwind. A solution to this is to run the downhaul through the pole as before but dead-end it in the boat at the back of the pole. A stopper knot is then put in the system which lets the spinnaker stow in the chute but still enables the act of pulling the spinnaker into the chute to also pull back the pole (Illustration 8.25).

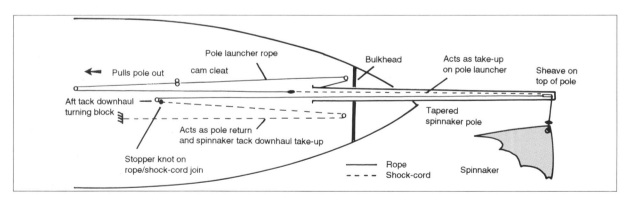

8.24: Pole launch system, seen from above looking down onto the boat. The pole is just short of fully extended. When the pole launch rope is pulled in the direction shown this pulls out the pole via the block mounted in the bulkhead. The slack on this rope is taken up by a piece of shock cord led up the inside of the pole and terminated in a stopper knot at the outside end of the pole. The pole is then held in place by the cam cleat. The action of pulling out the pole also launches the spinnaker tack out of the chute. It first takes up the slack in the tack downhaul rope till the stopper knot hits the aft block. And then pulls the spinnaker tack out of the chute through the sheave in the end of the pole. When the pole is fully out the tack downhaul rope is taut between the stopper knot on the fixed aft turning block and the spinnaker tack at the sheave in the end of the pole.

8.25: *In (a) we can see the tip of the pole sticking out of the bow with the spinnaker tack downhaul rope leading out of the sheave in the end of the pole. From there it goes back into the chute where it attaches to the spinnaker tack. The view in (b) is from above, as with 8.24. The spinnaker tack downhaul is dead-ended in the boat behind where the pole stows and when the pole is pulled out it launches the spinnaker. When the spinnaker is dropped, as the tack is pulled into the chute, the pole comes back with it when the stopper knot comes up tight against the underside of the sheave in the outer end of the pole. The subsequent slack in the spinnaker tack downhaul then just lies inside the pole or the pole sock.*

a

Stopper knot

Bulkhead

Pole launcher

Spinnaker tack downhaul

Sheave

Spinnaker tack

b

On boats such as the I14 a rather subtle take-up system is possible on the spinnaker halyard. Remember when the spinnaker is up, the retrieval line is the tail of the halyard so there is no loose rope to sort out before the drop. But when the spinnaker is down the excess rope now forms a loose bight which can wash around the double floor when going upwind and tie itself round everything. The take-up system is designed so that it goes slack when the pole is launched (Illustration 8.26)

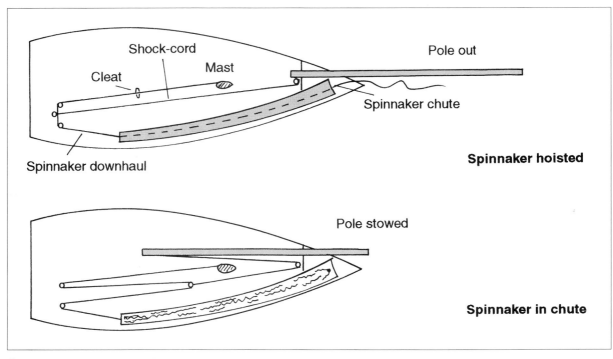

a

8.26: *Above in (a) the spinnaker is hoisted so the shock cord attached to the pole is slack, allowing the spinnaker halyard/downhaul to lead straight across the two turning blocks at the aft end of the boat. Below, as the pole is stowed and the spinnaker is in the chute the shock cord is pulled tight by the pole coming back. Which in turn takes up the slack in the spinnaker halyard/downhaul leading through the two turning blocks aft. In (b) we can see the halyard take-up shock cord turning through a block in the bulkhead with the pole fully extended. Note the darker pole launching rope turning round the block underneath.*

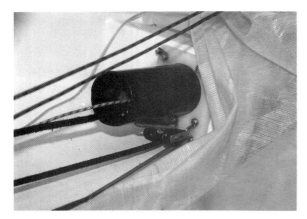

b

Chapter 9

Hull Fittings

The penultimate chapter is about the remaining equipment - that not concerned with sail or mast control. First in this category are the foils, rudder and centreboard.

Rudder

The first priority in the rudder fitting is setting it up both straight and central to the hull and rig. The comparison point for this exercise will be the centreboard case. This should project a properly fitted centreboard downwards exactly perpendicular to the hull. It can be checked before you fit the centreboard by using a long, flat, straight rod pushed against the side of the case and sticking out into the boat. Use a spirit level to check that the boat is exactly horizontal by laying a flat across between the shroud bases and then that the rod is exactly upright. If it is not then the boat builder has not done his job properly and the centreboard case may need realigning but assuming that it is correct you now have a vertical that the rudder can be lined up with.

To find the centrepoint of the transom, run a string from the stem fitting of the jib, aft to the transom. Find the point on the transom where it lies exactly in line with the centreboard case. If there is no such point then the centreboard is twisted in comparison to the centreline of the boat. But if you can find this point you will have the rudder in line with the centreboard. This is more important than measuring in from the gunwales at the back of the boat to find a centre. Dinghy transoms are sometimes not symmetric, and having rudder and centreboard in line both fore and aft and vertically is the priority. Once you have the centreline and the vertical, fixing the rudder to line up with them is no easy task. You must take enormous care before you drill the holes. It once took us six hours to fit a rudder to a 470 - but it was perfect when it was done.

The type of fittings you use to attach the

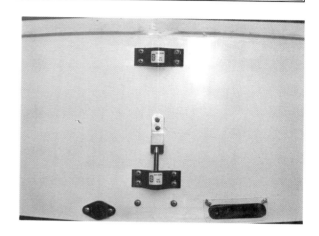

9.1: *Conventional pintle and gudgeon on the back of a 420.*

9.2: *Fixed rudder, this must be put in place in deep water so it requires greater boathandling skills than the retractable rudder.*

rudder stock will depend both on the class and whether you use a fixed or lifting blade. The conventional solution is the pintle and gudgeon (Illustration 9.1). The fixed blades are the lightest, strongest rudders (Illustration 9.2) incorporating stock, blade and fittings into one unit. The disadvantages are launching and

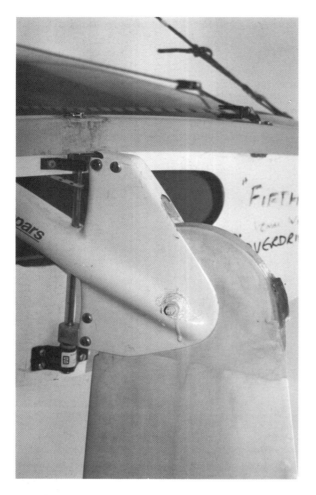

tail of which is visible above the tiller in Illustration 9.3. This tail leads over a pin in the rudder stock, then down to a cleat near the top of the rudder blade. It resists any attempt by the blade to kick back and up, which would rotate the top of the blade forward and down. But if you hit the ground it should be this that gives way, rather than the blade, stock or the transom of the boat. The other advantage of the lifting rudder is that it allows you to vary the angle of the blade with the windspeed. Rake vertically, or even slightly forward, in a breeze to reduce the feel, and rake back in light airs to increase the feel (and the cynical would add, rake half-up to row off the start line in big international fleets). But beware of class rules that forbid adjustment of the angle, like the 470 class.

However you fix the rudder to the boat, one important and often neglected job is keeping it there. The most common technique is the plastic or stainless clip (Illustration 9.4). This is the most secure method, if fitted properly so it locates far enough out over the gudgeon. But they can make it difficult to get the rudder on and off. This is not too much of a problem with a lifting rudder which can be removed on the shore, but it can prove a real liability with a fixed rudder. Which is why many people use the elastic hold downs on fixed rudder blades.

9.3: *A neat rudder fixing on the back of a 470; the stainless steel pin runs through the transom bar, and down through two gudgeons on both the rudder stock and the transom - this takes very careful fixing to get it all lined up, and straight!*

retrieving the boat, you have to be at least waist deep in water before you can get the rudder on. On lee shores you need to be able to sail the boat off the shore without it. Partly for these reasons some classes insist on lifting rudders. In which case the rudder fittings will depend on the design of the stock and the transom of the boat (illustration 9.3), and need not be a pintle and gudgeon.

With a lifting rudder you should pay great attention to holding the rudder down. At the minimum you will need a good 2:1 tackle, the

Tiller and Extension

Coming up from the rudder and stock is the tiller and extension. The tiller should be as long as possible, but still allow you to get between the end and the mainsheet if you have a centre main take-off. Aluminium is the best material as it is a lot more forgiving of abuse. You can sit on it, trip over it and be dragged behind the boat hanging on to it and, usually, it will only bend. The tiller extension joint is a critical fitting, and the rubber universal joints that have appeared in recent years are marvellous inventions compared to their stainless ancestors (Illustration 9.5). The major advantage is that they will not jam at any angle. With the metal ones it is possible to get the tiller extension locked in the upright position through a tack, with disastrous results when the boom

a

b

c

9.4: *The rudder retaining clip in (a) simply springs back into place over the top of the rudder stock fitting. In (b) the split ring prevents the pin pulling out, but you could never get this in place on the water with a fixed rudder. Instead you can use the elastic hold down in (c).*

came over and took the whole lot out of your hands.

Most extensions arrive from the shop with some type of grip. Our personal preference is the golf club style, but even these do not go far enough down the extension. There are a couple of ways of extending the grip, winding string round and gluing or taping it in place is one (Illustration 9.6), tape loops is another. A popular addition on trapeze boats is the telescopic extension (Illustration 9.7). This allows you to extend the tiller extension so that the crew can steer the boat from the wire. The idea being that the helm can do such jobs as clipping the pole on and tidying up after a messy or hurried spinnaker drop while the crew steers - keeping the maximum weight outboard and the boat going as fast as possible.

9.5: *Rubber universal tiller extension joint, check them regularly for cracking as they fail quickly once this starts to happen.*

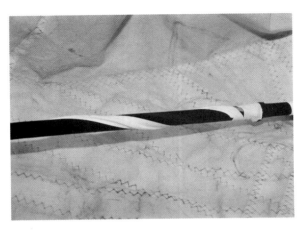

9.6: A good method for adding grip to the tiller extension, wind string round the tube and tape it in place.

9.7: A telescopic tiller extension, the extension is on a threaded lock, twist it to release, pull it out and twist to lock again.

Centreboards

Fitting the centreboard should be much more straightforward than the rudder. The one big possible complication is the use of a gybing board. These boards are held tight in the case only at the leading or trailing edge, the idea being that they pivot so that the leading edge moves up to windward. This increases the angle of attack of the board going upwind and so increases the lift generated. But it is not a project for the inexperienced. Too much twist will increase drag over the extra lift and slow you down. And if the board twists the wrong way it will pull you to leeward not windward! You will need the help of an experienced foil maker if you want to set this up.

Fortunately most classes ban the use of gybing boards and so your main task in fitting the system is being able to get the board up and down easily, without it flying up of its own accord when you want it down. At the same time there must be absolutely no movement (except flexing) of the tip when the board is fully extended. (The job of getting the board straight in the boat is down to the builder getting the case right - as we have explained above.) Getting just the right amount of friction between the centreboard and the case is half the job of the board moving properly. The best way to approach this is to get the board made a couple of millimetres thinner than the case

width. A good foil maker should be able to build to this accuracy. Then pack either the case or the foil with PTFE tape. This is sticky backed tape with a Teflon finish that is very low friction. It is the same material that they coat non-stick pans with. If you use this tape to pack the board tight into the case it will still move smoothly on its Teflon bearers whilst preventing any slop in the fit.

Rope systems for pulling the board up and down work off the head of the board. The questions are how much purchase to have in each direction, where to pull it from and whether to make it continuous. The amount of purchase you need will depend on how successful you have been in reducing friction in the case. If you need much more than a 3:1 you should probably look at this rather than increase the purchase, with a 4:1 you have to pull on a lot of rope to achieve any movement. A 2:1 usually works satisfactorily, but a 1:1 you may find a struggle. Where to pull it from depends on who is doing the pulling, the conventional method is to run the purchase up and down the centreboard case where it can be reached by the helm and the crew when in the boat. It can be led out to the side tank though, either forward near the shroud or aft for the helmsman. On the 505 the uphaul is often led to the shroud, the crew just heaves on it as he comes inboard at the windward mark. The downhaul is led to the helmsman so he can pull it down at the leeward mark as the crew is occupied with the spinnaker drop.

This raises the final question of whether or not the system should be continuous. We feel quite strongly that it should not as this means that the elastic take-up used to take the slack out of the system will be between you and the centreboard on either the uphaul or the downhaul. In other words you will have to pull about three feet of rope against the elastic before it comes up against the stops and you start to pull the centreboard. If you only have one hand this can cost you seconds every time you do it. It is far better to have two individual systems with the tails on separate elastic take-ups. Then as soon as you pull on them the board starts to move. If you use a 2:1 or 3:1 one armful will usually achieve what you require (Illustration 9.8).

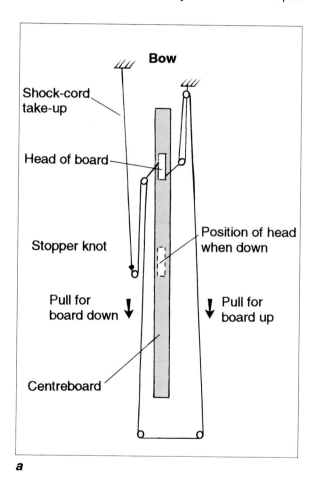

a

b

c

9.8: *Centreboard uphaul/downhaul systems, in (a) we have a continuous 2:1 purchase system. The big disadvantage of this is that on the downhaul you have to pull all the elastic slack out of the system before you move the board. The system in (b) is much better, with a 2:1 or 3:1 purchase on the head of the board and the tail run aft to an elastic take-up (c). The downhaul is on one side and the uphaul is on the other. You must be careful about the leads on the blocks, they have to be correct through the full range of the board's movement because you are always pulling against the friction in the opposing rope system as well as the friction in the case.*

Something that needs a great deal of attention is the slot gaskets - the cloth trim that is added to the bottom of the boat around the centreboard case to stop water flowing inside it. You have two choices here, either mylar or sailcloth. Many chandleries sell both the sail cloth and the mylar strip. The sailcloth versions need to be stretched out tight and held down quite strongly, perhaps with an aluminium strip. This can be a difficult job, and there is a considerable amount of work involved in fairing in the strip afterwards. But they will last for a long time once they are on. The alternative is glueing on mylar strips. This has the advantage of being a lot easier to do and provided the recess in the hull is the right height, it fits flush with almost no further effort. The disadvantage is that they do not last for long, and to be sure of not losing them during a race you will need to change them regularly. We once had to redo mylar slot gaskets three times in a week. The problem was that no glue would work on the Formica padding we had epoxied in to bring the recess up to the right height. The most interesting aspect was the volume of water that comes into the boat with no slot gaskets - if they fell off during a race you might as well go home. If you go the mylar strip route be prepared for a lot of maintenance, so you can be absolutely sure that by the time you get to a major regatta they are there to stay.

Often the key to doing a really good job is the front edge of the gasket that the board butts up against. Here you need the gasket to fit as tightly as it possibly can against the board. But with the mylar this can often start a split in the material which eventually destroys it. There are a couple of solutions. One is to use something like drysuit seal rubber at the front of the slot which will form closely round the board much more easily. Or you can punch a round hole in the mylar just where the board hits it, so it fits snugly (Illustration 9.9). A piece of polystyrene inserted into the bottom of the case inside the gaskets that the board butts up against will also do a good job.

One tip for fitting the centreboard into the case, when finding the hole to get the bolt through can be like searching for a needle in a haystack. Draw arrows on the board with a

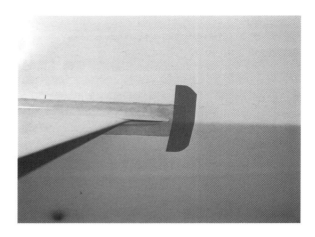

9.9: Mylar slot gaskets with additional brown tape to hold the leading edge in place. Note the small round hole at the front of the slot, to discourage the mylar from splitting.

9.10: Arrows pointing to the hole in a centreboard, to help you locate it when fitting it into the case - sight them through the pivot hole.

waterproof marker pointing towards the hole. Then all you have to do is move the board till you see one of the lines through the hole in the case, and follow it down until you pick up the hole in the board (Illustration 9.10).

Toe straps

On most boats the toe strap system requires minimum adjustment, once you have it right for your regular crew, that's it. Where you set them to will depend on the crew and the discomfort they are prepared to bear! The only rules are that they should be easy to pick up with your feet after a tack (Illustration 9.11). Suspending them with elastic is important, rather than solid fixings, otherwise if you tread on them you will rip them off their mountings. Make sure they are well padded too, as anything that helps keep the blood flowing to the feet will keep you sitting out that little bit longer. For a trapeze boat it is easier since you only need straps for the helmsman (Illustration 9.12).

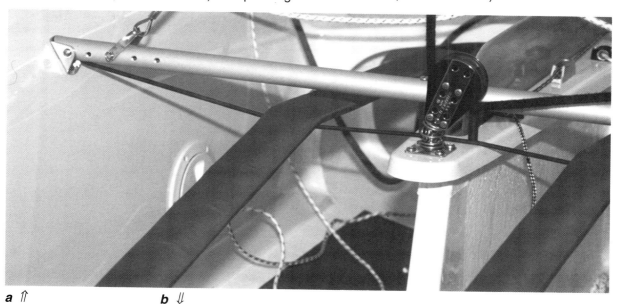

a ⇑   *b* ⇓

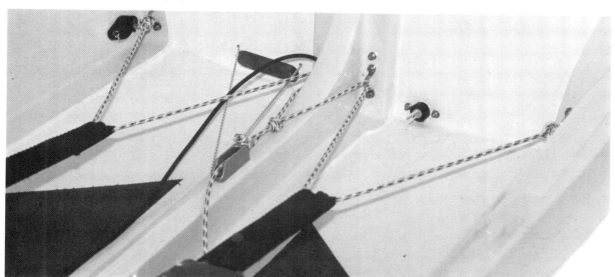

9.11: Toe straps in (a) suspended from the traveller bar. It is important that they are elasticated otherwise if you tread on them you will rip them off their fixings. In (b) we can see toe strap length adjustment on a 420.

9.12: *Toe straps fitted for the helmsman only, on a trapeze boat, it leaves the front of the cockpit much clearer for the crew.*

The Europe and Finn provide the most complex problem where you need to sit out at a different height depending on the wind angle you are sailing. Upwind you can get slumped over the edge with the straps really loose, but downwind you need them tighter to get your body out of the water. Since you can reduce the load on the straps easily by just flicking your weight off them, you do not need much purchase on these systems. A 2:1 rigged to the front of the strap with the cleat near to hand is usually adequate.

Trapezes

Trapezes provide more room for individuality, though the basic system is now almost standard (Illustration 9.13). It uses a 2:1 to raise or lower the height with a clam cleat to jam off

on. Any more than 2:1 and there will be too much string to tangle, round you, the hook and the sheets. If for some reason you are prevented from using this, perhaps by the class rules, then the two position hook provides at least some adjustment (Illustration 9.14).

The siting of the elastic retrieval is important. If it is too far forward and near the shroud the leeward wire will wrap itself around the shroud as soon as there is any breeze, and require freeing every time you tack. But in light airs having them placed aft severely hinders movement in and out of the boat when you are sitting forward. For this reason some crews have two positions for the retrieval, you clip it between the two depending on the breeze. The elastic retrieval should be strong and stretchy - so it holds the wire tight when not in use, but

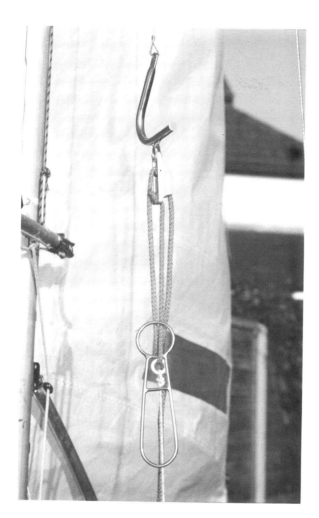

9.13: *Trapeze system, with a 2:1 adjustment and clam cleat. There is no pulley on the trapeze hook, which will make adjustment a lot harder.*

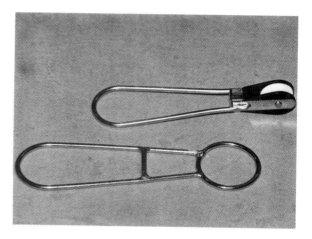

9.14: *Two trapeze hooks, the pulley at the top provides much better adjustment when used with a 2:1 system. The other version allows you to hook on at either the top or the bottom, giving you limited adjustment without a purchase system. This can be useful for trapezing helmsmen who may not have enough hands to use an adjustable system.*

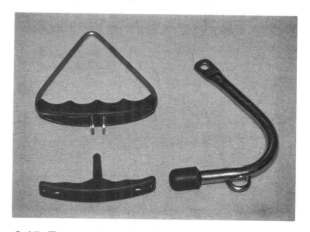

9.15: *Trapeze handles, the triangular version (top left) you have to put your hand through, which can be slow, but is comfortable. The bar across the wire (bottom left), which means getting the right number of fingers either side of the wire - slow and possibly uncomfortable. Or the karate chop (right), probably the most comfortable and the easiest to get hold of.*

allows the crew free movement aft when they need it. Run them to the back of the boat separately, rather than across the boat and joined. As well as more movement this means that if the elastic breaks you only have a problem with one trapeze.

The biggest area of individuality is the handle. The requirements are that you should be able to grab it quickly and easily to get your weight out fast, but also that it should be comfortable enough to hold onto while you clip on (Illustration 9.15). A recent trend is padding the wire above the adjustment system so that you can grab the wire itself. A tennis ball is then inserted at the join to the adjustment system to stop your hand sliding down the wire and off the end.

The other alternative is the continuous system, where you are always hooked onto an endless trapeze (Illustration 9.16). This is popular on boats with a genoa that is big enough to require two hands to sheet it in - on the Flying Dutchman it is standard. It also requires a high boom otherwise you will get fouled up with the vang on a pretty regular basis. The harness should be modified to ensure that the crew does not come off the hook accidentally, but at the same time he should be able to unclip quickly and easily in the event of a capsize.

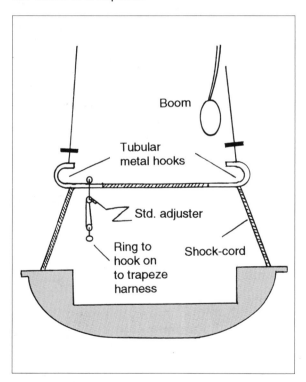

9.16: *Continuous trapeze system; the crew hooks onto the ring attached to the adjuster. This runs on a block between the metal hooks which are connected by shock cord - do not go out with the ring only as far as the shock-cord! You are free to tack with both hands on the genoa sheet.*

Compass

Compass mounting depends on who is assigned the job of watching it and how much you use it. Your choices are to centrally mount one compass, perhaps on the mast or on the deck by the mast gate (Illustration 9.17), or to put one either side (Illustration 9.18). Mounting two presents greater problems in the installation, since the compasses must exactly match. But with some of the modern designs on the market it can make the tactics a lot easier - providing you with a wind direction to watch rather than two headings.

The compass itself can be a difficult choice. It should at least be large enough to read easily, gimbaled so that when the boat is heeled fore and aft or sideways it stays level, and well-damped so that it does not jump around too much. The basic compass with its 360 degree card has been drowned in recent years by new designs for 'tactical' compasses. The central drive of these devices has been to provide just one number to remember rather than headings on each tack. They can do this two ways. One is to divide up the compass differently so that you read a number on one tack and the number plus 1 on the other tack. The disadvantage with this is that it divorces you from thinking about the compass heading, the windward mark bearing and their relationship to the forecast wind shifts. The other method is to have two compasses offset for each side of the boat. The compass ring is shifted 90 degrees so that you read a wind direction on each tack. But the compasses must be set up accurately otherwise they will not work. At the end of the day there is a lot to be said for being able to remember two headings properly!

a

b

c

9.17: Centrally mounted compasses, all these brackets came either from the builder or the compass manufacturer. They are all mounted on the boat so they are weighed with it. If you mount them on the mast, they are only part of an all-up weight, which only some classes have, but not part of the hull weight.

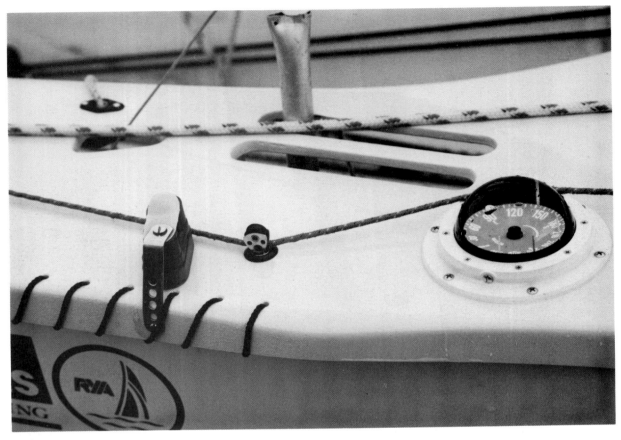

9.18: Sidetank mounted compass.

Bailers

Modern bailers are highly efficient, and provided they are fitted properly should give leak-free service, at least if they are stainless steel. The plastic versions have a tendency to break when trodden on - which is unfortunate for a fitting mounted on the floor! Fitting them flush is the difficult part and there never seems to be enough packing pieces to raise the flange (when it is on the inside of the hull) to get the outside surface of the bailer flush. What you can do in this situation is cut additional packing pieces out of mylar. These have the advantage of being thin so that you can raise it a small amount at a time, checking the hull with a ruler, until it is exactly right. When the flange is on the outside of the hull, usually the problem is reversed in that it will not recess far enough down. The only solution to this is to use a router

to cut the recess. If you do not have this kind of equipment either get a boat builder to fit it or buy the other sort of bailer.

If a bailer starts to leak after a period of otherwise sterling service you probably just need to replace the seal - contact the manufacturer or a chandlery (and hope it was not epoxied in). If you have a problem with dropping rope tails down them (which you should not if you have followed our advice on your control systems!) you can buy plastic grids to fit in the bailer mouth to stop this happening.

Grip

The addition of non-slip to gunwales and floors has moved on considerably with modern technology. Non-skid paint remains the best solution for the floors, you can either buy the product, mix sand in ordinary paint, or use epoxy hi-build with colloidal silica mixed in and stippled on. Another solution is to use sugar which can be dissolved out of the paint after it is

For the gunwale the trade-off is between good enough grip when trapezing, and so rough a surface that it destroys your clothes when sitting out. For this reason non-skids with solids in, like sand, should be avoided. The best solutions are the rubber strips, though these can be heavy and difficult to stick down, or stringing the gunwales. This is a difficult job to do well, but once done will last for the life of the

9.19: Wooden push-off pads in an International 14. This is the most positive way to lever yourself outboard when trapezing. Unfortunately many class rules forbid the addition of such equipment.

dry. This leaves a stippled finish which is not as harsh as sand. Another good solution is the stick-on strips of rubber material. These are excellent for small areas, especially in fibreglass boats, like thwarts that you use to push off when trapezing. Another possibility here is the addition of push off pads that give you positive grip (Illustration 9.19).

boat, by replacing the string. It provides the right combination of grip without excessive roughness (illustration 9.20).

113

a

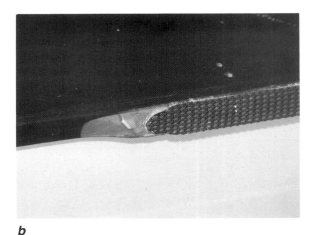

b

c

9.20: *Solutions to the problem of grip on the gunwale. In (a) non-slip paint has been done with epoxy hi-build and colloidal silica. In (b) a strip of rubber grip has been glued on. Note the rounded end, corners are always the first place that this material starts to peel off. In (c) holes have been drilled and string threaded through the gunwale. And on this 14 toe-loops have been added.*

Chapter 10

Rope and Wire

Rope

Synthetic fibre technology has improved to the extent where it is (almost) unnecessary to use anything but rope as the running rigging in a dinghy. And if class rules allow, it will soon eclipse wire for the standing rigging. But when you fit out your new control system with rope, you must chose the right material for the job, and make sure it is terminated correctly onto blocks and shackles. The first is not an easy task when you see the profusion of brand names in the rope section of any chandlery.

Materials

A good place to start is the basic properties of the chemical substances that the ropes are made from. The five modern manufacturing materials are polypropylene, nylon, polyester, aramid, and high modulus polyethylene (HMPE). They are used either on their own, or combined with one of the others to produce a composite rope with properties for a specific job. Much in the same way that you would combine resin systems with carbon, Kevlar, Nomex and foam to build hulls of exactly the right weight, cost and strength, so the rope manufacturers combine their five materials to provide exactly the right rope for a particular job.

First there is polyester, which we more commonly know by the trade name of Dacron, and find in sails as well as ropes. Although it cannot compete with the more exotic materials, it is still a good low-stretch, high-strength fibre with excellent weather and abrasion resistance. As such it is one of the best materials for the cover of a rope, as well as doing good service in a lot of applications where weight and stretch are not critical.

Nylon, by comparison, is a high-stretch, high-strength fibre that would be completely inappropriate for a vang, but would work as a tow or anchor line where it is light and absorbs the energy from shock loading. Whereas polypropylene has only about 60 per cent of the strength of nylon and polyester and so has little to recommend it as a working rope. Its big redeeming quality is that it does not absorb water, and if used in the right places can considerably reduce the wet weight of the boat.

Then there is the aromatic polyamide fibre, or aramid, which is better known by the brand name of Kevlar. This is a very low-stretch, high-strength fibre, with the same chemical base as nylon, but with additional molecules that make the structure more rigid. Whilst this gives the material its enormous strength, as well as the ability to withstand temperatures up to 500 degrees, it is also the cause of its biggest defect. The material is weak when point loaded because of the rigid molecular structure, so the sheaves it runs round must have a bigger radius and the knotted strength is markedly reduced. In addition, it has poor UV and abrasion resistance, which necessitates being covered by another material, usually polyester, which in some situations adds markedly to the weight of rope required for the job.

Last, but certainly not least, is high modulus polyethylene, or HMPE, which is sold under the two trade names of Spectra and Dyneema. Again this is a particularly low-stretch and high-strength fibre, and although it is basically the same material that you use to carry your shopping home, the grade of polyethylene used in ropes is vastly superior stuff. The molecules are longer and when spun they are all aligned along the length of the filaments. It is this molecular construction that gives HMPE its biggest advantage over the aramids: it can be point loaded. It is also much more weather and abrasion resistant. Its weaknesses are that it is slippery, so you have to design the rope carefully to avoid the cover sliding against the core, but more significant is its propensity to creep. By this we mean that the rope extends if it is left under constant high loading. So whatever it was that you tightened with the rope gradually gets looser.

Dyneema and Spectra are chemically the same material, the difference is that they are made by two separate companies with two different processes; *Allied Fibres* make Spectra in the United States and *D.S.M.* make Dyneema in Holland for the European market. The HMPE rope that you buy in the U.S. is almost exclusively Spectra, whereas in Europe it is Dyneema. The differences in performance, of stretch and strength, between the two are slight, and with both manufacturers constantly searching for ways to improve the product the quality balance is always shifting.

Construction

The next big variant in rope manufacture is who made it from the yarn, and how. The quality of the rope for a given job will depend as much on how the rope is constructed as on what it was made from. Different manufacturers have different processes, many of which are patented. But one of the common methods of improving the rope is pre-stretching and heat setting. This means stretching the yarn at an elevated temperature, and it can be done at any stage of manufacture. The idea is to take out the initial stretch in the fibre, and because of the temperature, set this extension into the yarn. It produces a stiffer yarn, so the rope will have a harder finish, as well as being lower stretch.

The traditional way of making a rope is by twisting the yarn into strands, and then winding three strands into a rope (Illustration 10.1). This three-strand construction, whilst easily spliced, stretches more and kinks much more easily than the core/cover ropes. It also works poorly in jammers, which is why we find the two-part construction everywhere in the sail handling systems of a modern dinghy.

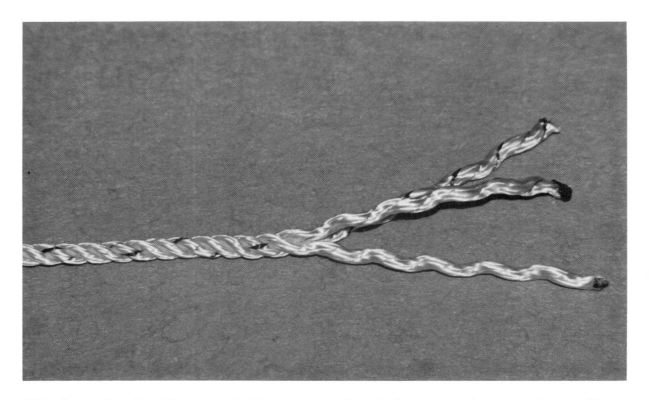

10.1: Conventional 3 plait rope, notice that each strand has had the end sealed to stop it unravelling. This is worth doing before you attempt to splice it.

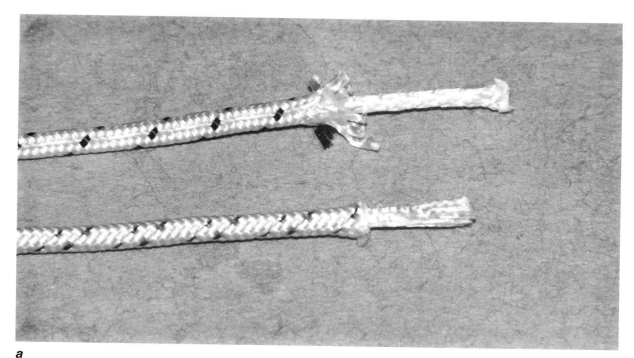

a

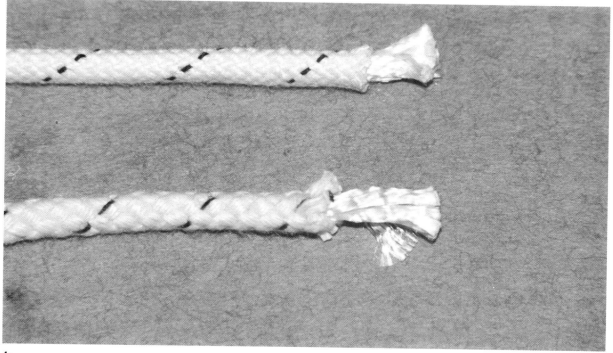

b

10.2: *Some two-part cordage. In (a) we have Dacron rope with a 3 ply core and 16 plait cover (top) and 8 plait cover (bottom). In (b) we have HMPE (top) and Kevlar (bottom).*

There are variations on the core/cover theme, each of which has its pros and cons. The core can be either the three-strand construction described above, a braided weave or aligned in parallel. When considering the core the parameters are that the less twisted the fibres are from the line of the load, i.e. along the rope, the stronger the rope will be in a straight pull. So, the parallel lay up is the strongest, followed by the three-strand and then the braided core. A further problem for the braided core is the extra abrasion between the yarns.

The disadvantage of the parallel construction is that it is weaker when it runs around bends, as the load is unequally shared amongst the strands. This is a bigger problem for the low stretch fibres, Spectra and Kevlar, than for Dacron ropes where the fibres stretch until they take up the load more evenly. The three strand can be seen as a useful compromise between parallel and braided lay-ups, being not quite as strong in a straight pull as the parallel core, but superior round bends; compared to the braided core its position is reversed, stronger in a straight pull but weaker round bends. Which is the more appropriate construction will depend on the application.

The rope covers are always braided, with an 8 or 16-plait construction: the more plaits there are the more rounded the rope and the tighter the finish. This affects how it handles, runs round blocks, jams in cleats and so on. The yarn type is important for the cover. There are two sorts, spunstaple yarns which are made from short lengths, or filaments, of the material, and continuous filament yarns where the individual filaments are as long as the length of the rope. The continuous yarns are stronger, for obvious reasons, and will always be used in the core. But often spunstaple makes a better cover since it has a matt, almost hairy, feel with plenty of friction, compared to the shiny finish of continuous yarn covers (Illustration 10.2).

Uses

So, given this mountain of information on rope technology, what is the best rope? It depends on the use, and for those of us not involved in limitless budget Olympic campaigns, cost. For a halyard the initial choice would seem to be Kevlar, as the propensity of Spectra to creep under a fixed load would mean constant readjustment. But Kevlar is prone to breaking on sheaves and terminations. So Spectra stays in the frame for the job, and has one other advantage - you can remove the cover in areas where it will not be used in a jammer. This is because Spectra, like polyester, nylon and polypropylene, is resistant to UV, where Kevlar is not. The braided polyester cover used to prevent Kevlar degrading adds considerably to the weight of rope required compared to the stripped Spectra equivalent.

But now you have to get around or live with the creep problem. Perhaps using a halyard lock on the mainsail, so that the load is taken off the halyard once the sail is raised. The spinnaker is only up for twenty minutes or so at a time, and is not a problem. But with the jib halyard the need for accurate rig calibration makes the use of Spectra impossible. And because it is holding the rig up Kevlar's weakness at the terminations makes it a risky choice. This is one place where you may have to stick to wire.

But what if cost is factored into the decision? For a finished halyard Spectra, Kevlar and wire are all similar prices. But for the mainsheet, which is both constantly adjusted and right in the middle of the boat where the weight is concentrated, Dacron is a good alternative. It is a lot cheaper for areas where low stretch and weight are not an absolute priority. Similarly there is more than one sort of Dacron rope around, should you go for the more expensive parallel cored version or the cheaper braided rope? The answer should be provided by how many corners the rope must negotiate. The cover is important too, spunstaple covers handle better, but get chewed up faster by ratchet blocks and jammers - you trade handling for less frequent replacement.

Once you have selected the type of rope, you need to choose the diameter. The load is obviously important, it should be capable of withstanding the same forces as the blocks you have used. So is the size of block and cleat that you have. If the line is too thin it will jump blocks, and not jam properly. If it is too thick it will not run smoothly or fit in jammers. The handling is also important, too thin a line can be impossible to hold onto for any length of time.

One technique that is commonly used on sheets to overcome this problem is tapering. There are several ways of doing it, but essentially you use thin rope in the areas of a jib, spinnaker or mainsheet that are never handled, with a thicker rope in the sections that are. One way of achieving this is to use a thin rope for the whole sheet, then pull a thicker cover over the top of it and stitch it in place. Alternatively you can buy specially made ropes with two covers (Illustration 10.3) or splice together the thick and thin sections.

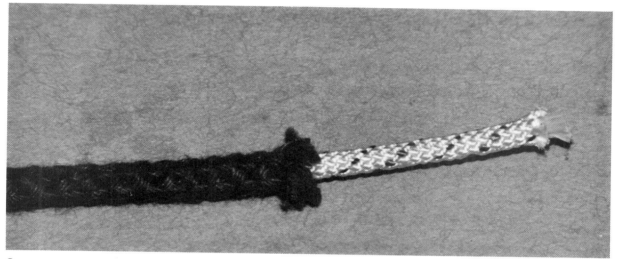

a

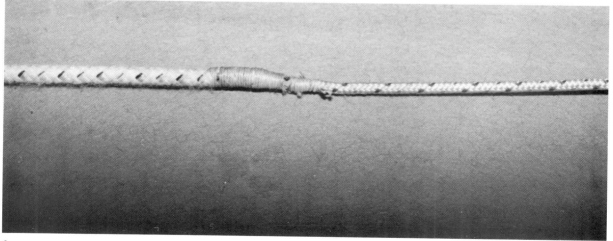

b

10.3: Tapered sheets; you can buy the rope with two covers. In (a) you can see the Kevlar core, with a 16 plait continuous filament cover, then a further 8 plait spunstaple cover. In (b) we see the finished sheet, with the outside cover peeled back off the areas that are not handled. The spunstaple cover provides a good, comfortable grip on the sections that are held, and the continuous filament cover is hard wearing on the areas that go round the blocks.

119

The techniques of splicing modern multi-plait ropes are mostly restricted to the few professionals who specialise in them. But you can do a reasonably good job by pulling the core out of the thick rope, chopping 8 inches off, then stitching it onto the end of the thinner rope and pulling the join back inside the cover of the thick rope. Finish by stitching through the whole rope along the length of the spliced section.

A similar technique can be used to construct two-part ropes to save both cost and weight. A good example is the mainsheet, where the last few metres of the tail is not subjected to much load. In fact all the Dacron tail does for 60% of the race is lie in the bottom of the boat soaking up water. What you can do to minimise the weight that this adds, is to splice on a section of polypropylene that is both light and does not absorb water. Although it is not as strong as Dacron or Spectra, it will only ever be used when broad reaching or running when the mainsheet loads are much below those upwind.

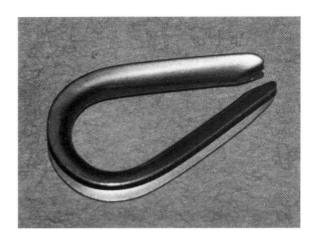

10.4: Metal eye that can be used to spread the load when you are terminating Kevlar.

All wire used on racing dinghies should be of stainless steel strands. It can be either stiff, for standing rigging, or flexible, for use when it runs through blocks. The lay-up and construction is varied to produce the appropriate properties. There are four basic constructions and three termination techniques, these are shown in illustration 10.5.

Termination

Because of the problem of splicing them, terminating modern rope is best done with a bowline. If you are worried about it coming undone, stitch the end of the rope to the main part and that will keep it together. Sometimes it is worth putting a plastic or metal eye in the termination, to spread the point load around the rope surface (Illustration 10.4). This is particularly important for Kevlar, and if you have to use this material you should always use a hard eye on the termination.

Wire

Although for almost all the running rigging the modern synthetic fibres provide a lighter, more user friendly option than wire, there are still some places where it is useful - the jib halyard for instance. It is also the most common standing rigging material, partly because of class rules. But also because, whilst the fibre alternatives exist, they are as yet relatively unproven.

120

a

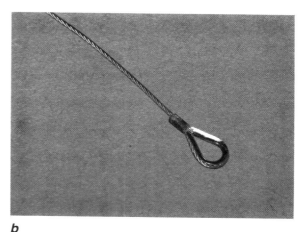

b

c

10.5: *Wire termination, in (a) we have a soft eye, where a loop in the wire is secured by a ferrule. It is used on halyards or other places where the end must pass through a slot or sheave. In (b) we have a hard eye, where the loop in the wire is lined with a stainless steel thimble secured by a ferrule. This is used where the wire is attached to any fixing. The thimble prevents the wire taking up too tight a radius. The terminals in (c) are attached to the wire by swaging, which is controlled crushing onto the wire. This is the only way to terminate some types of wire. From the right we have: a standard eye terminal; a fork terminal; a tee-terminal which fits into matching tee-shaped slots - used in masts for shrouds, trapeze wires etc.; and a hook terminal which is similar to the tee-terminal but is not as secure when not under load (anyone who has hoisted their mainsail, caught it under a hook terminated trapeze wire and pulled it straight out of the mast will know all about this).*

121

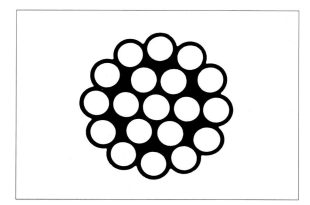

10.6: Viewed from the end, this is the construction of 1x19 wire.

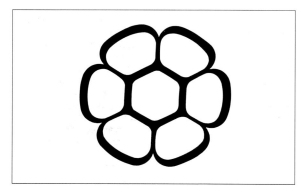

10.7: Viewed from the end, this is the construction of 1x7 Dyform wire.

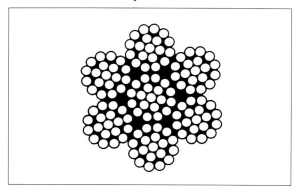

10.8: Viewed from the end, this is the construction of 7x19 wire.

The most common standing rigging wire is 1x19 construction (Illustration 10.6). This is stiff wire, relatively low stretch and easy to terminate. It can be terminated with soft eyes, hard eyes or any swaged end. It is used in shrouds, forestays, strops and trapeze wires. Its advantages are lower cost, ease of termination and fairly long life, but it is not the lowest stretch option.

There are two lower stretch wire types commonly available. The first is 1x7 Dyform. This is a recently developed wire built in seven strands which are then passed through a die to form and compact the wire into the cross-section in illustration 10.7. This gives a higher density of metal for the cross-sectional area, and hence higher strength and lower stretch when compared to 1x19 construction of the same diameter. In general this is the best wire for shrouds and forestays as it gives the best stretch and strength characteristics for a given diameter. Often because of this you can use a size smaller than conventional 1x19 and this can also give a weight saving. The only disadvantage is that you must use swage ends to terminate it, which involves specialized tools.

If you really want low stretch, then the ultimate solution is rod. But the development of Dyform has seen this drop in popularity as it is much more difficult to handle and is prone to failure without warning if it becomes kinked or nicked.

None of the above will travel round blocks, so for applications like the vang you need 7x19, which has the cross sectional construction shown in illustration 10.8. It will probably be superseded by HMPE for these kinds of applications however. The construction is such that for a given overall diameter the size of each individual strand is much smaller and so is more willing to negotiate turnings such as blocks. Although more expensive than 1x19 it can be used on trapeze wires where it has more stretch and so can withstand more shock loading when, for example, the boat takes off over a wave. As with 1x19 any type of termination may be used.

Most wire failures occur where the wire has been chafed or kinked, so it is important to regularly inspect for broken strands. The only remedy here is to replace the wire in question and prevent the damage recurring.

Index

Appendix A.
Units of Measure

Linear
1in = 25.4mm = 2.54cm
1in = 0.083ft
1ft = 12in = 30.48cm
6ft = 1 fathom
1 statute mile = 5280ft
1 statute mile = 1.6093km

1mm = 0.03937in
1cm = 0.3937in
1m = 39.37in = 3.2809ft
1 fathom = 1.8288m
1 nautical mile = 6080ft
1km = 0.6214 statute mile

Area
1sq in = 6.4516sq cm
1sq ft = 144sq in
1sq ft = 0.0929sq m

1sq cm = 0.1550sq ft
1sq in = 0.00108sq ft
1sq m = 10.764sq ft

Weight
1oz = 28.35gr
1oz = 0.02835kg
1lb = 16oz
1lb = 453.6gr = 0.4536kg

1gr = 0.03527oz
1kg = 35.274oz
1oz = 0.0625lb
1kg = 2.2046lb

Pressure
1lb per sq in = 0.0703kg per sq cm
1kg per sq cm = 14.223lb per sq in

Power
1000 watts = 1 kilowatt = 1.34 horsepower
1 horsepower = 747 watts

Appendix B.
General Characteristics of Synthetic Marine Rope Materials

	Nylon	Polyester (Dacron)	Polypropylene	Aramid (Kevlar)
Strength	strong	strong	strong	very strong
Stretch	stretches	low-stretch	low-stretch	low-stretch
Shrinkage	shrinks	low-shrink	low-shrink	no shrink
Flotation	sinks	sinks	floats	sinks
Cost	moderate	moderate	cheap	high
Common Uses	mooring and docking lines	sheets and halyards	water ski towlines	running rigging

Appendix C.
Quick Guide to Strength of Rope Materials

	Diameter in Inches of 3-Strand or Double-Braid Nylon Rope											
	1/16	1/8	3/16	1/4	5/16	3/8	7/16	1/2	5/8	3/4	7/8	1
Diameter in Millimeters	1.5	3	5	6	8	9	11	13	16	19	22	25
Braid Size	2	4	6	8	10	12	14	16	20	24	28	32
Circumference in Inches	3/16	3/8	5/8	3/4	1	1⅛	1¼	1½	2	2¼	2¾	3
Weight in Feet Per Pound	400	200	100	65	40	30	20	16	10	7	5	4
Breaking Strength in Pounds	200	400	750	1000	2000	3000	4000	6000	10000	17000	20000	25000

Polypropylene – 20 percent lighter in weight than nylon; 20 percent weaker.

Polyester – 20 percent heavier than nylon; about same strength.

Aramid (Kevlar) – 40 percent heavier than nylon; 200 percent stronger.

Note: This chart is for 3-strand and double-braid rope of the same weight and quality. The safe working load of rope is about 10 percent of its breaking strength. In **ALL** critical situations, consult the manufacturer's load recommendations.

Appendix D.
Weights and Strengths of Wire Ropes

Diam	1x7 galv. iron seizing strand		1x7 annealed s.s. seiz. strand		7x7 galv. improved plow steel		7x19 galv. improved plow steel		7x7 s.s. 302/304		7x19 s.s. 302/304		1x19 s.s. 302/304	
	strength (lbs)	wt/ 1000ft	strength (lbs)	wt/ 1000ft	strength (lbs)	wt/ 1000ft	strength (lbs)	wt/ 1000ft	strength (lbs)	wt/ 1000ft	strength (lbs)	wt/ 1000ft	strength (lbs)	wt/ 1000ft
1/16	140	10	230	8.5	480	7.5			480	7.5			500	8.5
3/32	300	20	500	20	920	16	1000	16	920	16	920	16	1200	20
1/8	540	33	900	33	1700	28.5	2000	29	1700	28.5	1760	29	2100	35
5/32	870	50	1350	50	2600	43	2800	45	2400	43	2400	45	3300	55
3/16	1150	73			3700	62	4200	65	3700	62	3700	65	4700	77
7/32					4800	83	5600	86	4800	83	5000	86	6300	102
1/4					6100	106	7000	110	6100	106	6400	110	8200	135
9/32					7400	134	8000	139	7600	134	7800	139	10300	170
5/16					9200	167	9800	173	9000	167	9000	173	12500	210
3/8					13300	236	14400	243	12000	236	12000	243	17500	300
7/16*					NA		17600	356	15600	342	16300	356	22500	410
1/2*					NA		22800	458	21300	440	22800	458	30000	521
9/16*									26600	550	28500	590	36200	670
5/8*									32500	680	35000	715	47000	855

* IWRC in 7x19